European Commission

Martin Bangemann
Member of the Commission

Carole Tongue, MEP
Rapporteur on the European Car Industry

FORUM ON THE EUROPEAN AUTOMOBILE INDUSTRY
BRUSSELS — PALAIS DES CONGRÈS — 1 MARCH 1994

WRITTEN PROCEEDINGS

Conference Secretariat: Mr R. Wright - DG III/E/5 - European Commission -
N-9 3/29, 200 Rue de la Loi, - 1049 Brussels - tel.: (+32) 2 - 296.01.43; fax.: (+32) 2 - 296 96 37

Foreword

The European Commission and the European Parliament joined forces to organise a Forum on the European Automobile Industry to provide a platform to discuss key challenges facing the industry. The restructuring process in the industry was examined in detail as well as the responses of the various actors - employers, trade unions and public authorities including the Union - to the transformations underway. The effects of restructuring at regional level and the management of these changes were also discussed. The final workshop examined ways to enhance partnership and co-operation in the industry and among the Social Partners concerned.

The conference consisted of four workshops following the same format:

- A short introduction by the moderator;

- Speeches from the workshop's main speakers;

- An open discussion involving the whole panel, chaired by the moderator. This included questions from the floor;

- A short speech by the moderator summing up the workshop.

In addition, there was an opening address given by Mr Martin Bangemann, a Member of the European Commission, and Professor Roger Blanpain of the Law Faculty of the Catholic University of Leuven gave an independent summary speech to close the Forum.

TABLE OF CONTENTS

FORUM ON THE EUROPEAN AUTOMOBILE INDUSTRY

BRUSSELS · PALAIS DES CONGRÈS - 1 MARCH 1994

OPENING ADDRESS

MR MARTIN BANGEMANN
MEMBER OF
THE EUROPEAN COMMISSION

Good morning, ladies and gentlemen.

The European automobile industry is in the middle of a process of structural adjustment. The economic climate has clearly deteriorated. After years which saw ever-increasing record levels of new registrations, European manufacturers have had to come to terms since mid-1992 with declining volumes of sales. In 1993 sales virtually collapsed on a scale not experienced even since the first oil crisis in 1974.

Last year, new registrations in the EC fell by nearly 16%. The situation is therefore serious. However, we do not believe that this fall in demand will continue over the long term. Industry is facing a particularly serious cyclical crisis.

67,000 jobs were lost in the European automobile industry in 1993 alone, and an estimate of 100,000 losses for the industry as a whole, including suppliers, is probably not too high.

1993 was also the first major test for the agreement with Japan on Japanese car exports. The agreement passed this test. As provided for in the agreement, Japanese exports were pushed back more than proportionately by 18.4%. If European automobile manufacturers had had to bear the full brunt of the poor market situation on their own, the labour market would inevitably have been hit far worse. My staff came back last weekend from the latest round of talks with the MITI in Tokyo. For the first time, the differences between our estimates of the market are only very small. While the Commission assumes that demand in the Union will remain more or less constant, Japan still believes there will be very slight growth.

An initial exchange of views on levels of exports for 1994 has taken place. We want to continue these talks as soon as possible to achieve results which will enable European and Japanese industry to do reliable planning.

The only positive trend last year was in exports. Exchange rate fluctuations along with more aggressive marketing and, in particular, the production of better and cheaper vehicles by European manufacturers helped the Union in 1993 once again to export more cars and commercial vehicles than it imported. However, this satisfactory result does not change the fact that European automobile producers are still clearly under-represented in the future growth markets. More direct investment outside the Union will not cost European jobs (delocalization) but, on the contrary, will safeguard jobs with high value-added and the financial stability of European manufacturers.

The crisis in the automobile market will not get any worse in 1994. The critical period has bottomed out. The first signs of improvement can be seen in some countries.

1994 will most certainly not be a good year for the industry but, to put it positively, it promises not to be as bad as 1993. Real growth is not expected to begin until 1995.

The weakness of demand at the moment is not the only challenge for the European automobile industry. There is still a need for structural adjustment. A key role in this respect is played by suppliers to the European automobile industry who, in terms of value-added per hour worked, are still way behind the Japanese supply industry. Further concentration on the most efficient suppliers therefore seems unavoidable. Conversely, however, this also requires a willingness to accept genuine partnership which will allow close co-operation in the development of new and cheaper components.

The European automobile industry's period of grace runs out in 1999. The structural adjustment must have been made by then. I am confident that the time available to make adjustment will not be wasted. Prime responsibility for the necessary structural change rests with manufacturers themselves. However, the two sides of industry also bear a large burden of responsibility for maintaining and strengthening Europe's position as a location for automobile production. Further increases in productivity are absolutely essential to remain internationally competitive and to prevent production being moved abroad.

The crucial factor in safeguarding Europe's position is to increase the efficiency of labour. This requires better trained staff and a willingness to accept teamwork. Achieving this is not only a question of cost but also a management problem. It is not only unyielding trades unions which have endangered jobs in the past by making excessive wage claims and refusing to accept flexible working hours but also unyielding managers who still think far too hierarchically.

How can the necessary structural change be supported through industrial policy?

The Union can intervene at three levels to help make the adjustment more easily:

- by focusing on the completed single market;
- by assisting in making the structural change needed;
- by increasing the rate of innovation.

Firstly: focusing on the completed single market

Completion of the single market has at last provided the European automobile industry with the long awaited, strong home market.

Major progress was made in 1993 by introducing EC type approval, which becomes compulsory from 1996. The new vehicle emission standards which come into force in 1996 will also further improve the stability of planning and give a new technological boost, which will make European cars more competitive in all world markets. The development of new standards to increase the active and passive safety of vehicles is expected to have the same effect.

The single market for cars is and will remain an open market. Mergers between European car firms or suppliers must therefore be assessed in a different way than in a closed market. Competition policy must not be based on abstract ideals. If, therefore, we are talking about deciding how the Block Exemptions Regulation will be applied in future, I am, of course, in favour of taking due account of the well-understood consumer interest. This also covers skilled servicing of cars, which are becoming an increasingly complex product, and making a choice from among a large range of models. Personally,

I do not believe that abolishing the selective, exclusive system of distribution will lead to more choice and lower prices, but rather the contrary.

The Commission is currently studying how the Regulation functions in detail, and how it can be further improved.

The contribution of the selective, exclusive system of distribution to the efficient operation of the agreement between the EU and Japan on foreign trade in cars will also be taken into account. In no circumstances must the agreement be put at risk.

Secondly: assisting in making the structural change needed

Every job in industry in the EC today is potentially in danger, particularly in the automobile industry. Increasing automation, better working methods and leaner production have meant that more and more jobs have been lost since 1980, even if not on the spectacular scale we have now been experiencing since 1992. We must therefore do our utmost to avoid any further rapid loss of jobs in this important sector of industry on which entire regions depend. In particular, we must make it easier for structural change to take place.

A key factor in this respect is, as I said earlier, improving employee qualifications. Spending money on training is always better than paying it out as unemployment benefit.

Further training must be improved so that employees are able to meet the increasing demands made within companies. Modern industrial organization requires a new type of employee who must bear more responsibility himself. In industrial operations, individuals must themselves recognize what is needed and must also be given responsibility for solving problems. The excessively rigid hierarchical structures we have had until now have often had the opposite effect. Instead of responsibility being exercised, the decision is passed up to the next highest level. This hinders the necessary flexibility and blocks openness to accept new production methods.

We know enough about these causes and effects. What we must jointly ensure is that our knowledge is put into practical effect on a broad front. This is the background to the recently introduced Objective 4 of the Community's Structural Fund and the ADAPT initiative. This is the framework in which joint funding will be provided for the further training and retraining of workers threatened by unemployment. A total of ECU 3.4 billion is available for the period 1994 to 1999, ECU 3 billion of this outside the Objective 1 areas alone. The joint programme for SMEs provides for additional funding of ECU 1 billion from which small and medium-sized suppliers in particular are able to benefit.

So there is enough money available. Everything now depends above all on the automobile industry's ability to devise projects which qualify for support and the willingness of the Member States to set aside funds for these projects. The European Commission has done its homework.

Thirdly: Increasing the rate of innovation

Another important way of strengthening the competitiveness of the European auto-mobile industry is through R&D policy. For example, the time between the designing of a car and its being ready for sale can be greatly reduced by using the latest, computer-as-sisted production methods. A timesaving of just one month means a saving of about ECU 30 billion when developing a new vehicle. Similar cost savings can be made through research into new production methods, which will be a major component of the factory of the future.

The fourth research framework programme has a total budget of about ECU 13 billion and contains a number of special programmes which will be of major importance for the European automobile industry, such as those concerning:

- industrial technologies;

- information technologies;

- environmental protection including transport.

The automobile industry benefited either directly or indirectly from about 10% of the funds under the third framework programme, impressive proof of how much modern technology is being put into cars. The automobile industry is a technological sector with a future ahead of it and one in which we must not in any circumstances allow ourselves to fall behind at international level.

It is therefore important to create strategic groups of individual research projects to optimize their benefit for the automobile industry. This requires close agreement with the industry, which has already begun. We have the same objectives as the US Government with its NGV programme, namely the low-cost production of "intelligent" cars with low emissions. The path we are taking is a different one, and I think a better one, since we are giving more support to "generic" technologies, which are beneficial in a number of different ways. However, the danger is that too much attention is paid to detail and not enough to the overall concept. The horizontal approach must not lead to support being given in all areas in an attempt to satisfy all demands while failing to take account of the real needs of the market. Strategic goals such as "clean cars" must be clearly defined and then put into practice in a concerted manner. Otherwise R&D policy will not make any effective contribution to increasing competitiveness.

Cars and the European automobile industry have a promising future. Cars are still the "first choice" as a means of transport. The automobile market is therefore still a growth market. Our assumption is that demand for new cars in the Union will rise by an average of more than 4% a year up to the year 2000, and that the increase in production will be slightly greater still if we produce cars which satisfy the highest demands in terms of environmental compatibility and safety. As far as environmental compatibility is concerned, the limits to the "passive" reduction of emissions, e.g. through the use of catalytic converters, have largely been reached. Further progress can only be made by means of a "multiple approach" aimed at the following:

- drive technology;
- forms of energy;
- transport systems.

The car of the future must meet continually rising environmental requirements, not least because of the rising levels of traffic in Europe. Advanced drive systems, for example, can help to reduce fuel consumption by a substantial amount. Research aimed at minimizing pollutant emissions is just as important. This is necessary to maintain society's acceptance of cars. We must also increase our efforts to create an efficient, environmentally acceptable transport system. All means of transport must be more closely interconnected. Roads, rail and air transport have their specific advantages which must be combined in an integrated European transport system.

We must not pursue policies which alienate consumers. Although last year was poor, consumers nevertheless clearly expressed their preference for cars as a means of transport by buying nearly 12 million new cars.

In whatever we do, it is essential to improve the dialogue between politicians and the automobile industry, including those who work in it and those who buy its products. Our aim must be to work together in devising ambitious but realistic goals for both our products and our performance.

Thank you very much.

FORUM ON THE EUROPEAN AUTOMOBILE INDUSTRY

BRUSSELS - PALAIS DES CONGRÈS - 1 MARCH 1994

WORKSHOP 1

THE EU CAR INDUSTRY
- BARRIERS TO RESTRUCTURING -
- SETTING THE SCENE -

Moderator:	Mr R. Perissich	Director General for Industry, European Commission
The EU Automotive Producers	Mr G. Garuzzo	President of the European Car Manufacturers Association, the ACEA, and President of Fiat Auto SpA
The Specific Situation of Component Suppliers	Mr E.K. Planchon	President of the European Automotive Suppliers Association, the CLEPA, and Director of International Affairs at Valeo SA
The View of Labour	Mr W. Jordan, CBE	President of the European Metalworkers' Federation, and President of the British Amalgamated Engineering and Electrical Union
Panel:	Mr I. McAllister	Chairman of Ford of Britain
	Mr P. Lepoutre	President of CECRA, the European Committee for Motor Trades and Repairs
	Mr H. Neumann	IG-Metall

📖 *Mr Perissich:*

Thank you Mr Bangemann. We will now start the first workshop. This workshop will focus on the barriers to restructuring in the car industry of the European Union, and will set the scene for the Forum, providing the background against which the other workshops will elaborate on more operational issues. We have three key speakers for this workshop: Mr Garuzzo, President of the European Car Manufacturers' Association, the ACEA, and President of Fiat Auto SpA; Mr Planchon, President of the Automotive Suppliers' Association, the CLEPA, and Director of International Affairs at Valeo S.A.; and Mr Jordan, CBE, President of the European Metalworkers' Federation and also President of the British Amalgamated Engineering and Electrical Union.

We want to leave some time at the end of the workshop for a question and answer session, and I would therefore be most grateful for concise contributions. I would request the principal speakers to restrict themselves to a maximum of ten minutes, and the other panellists to five minutes please.

📖 *Mr Garuzzo:*

The Importance of the European Automobile Industry

The car and truck manufacturers of Europe are well aware of the role and the importance of the industry for the economy and welfare of the continent, and are engaged in major development and restructuring work to keep it that way for the future.

Today the European automobile industry is soundly placed in the worldwide context and there is no doubt of its ability to maintain this position by constantly updating products and processes.

Criticism may be made on various accounts and actually has been made occasionally, but this underlying reality cannot be denied.

Since the first steps were taken towards the creation of a united Europe, the automobile industry has given its support to complete free trade within the continent. While other sectors, even some of considerable importance, are only now taking their first steps beyond traditional national frontiers, European car manufacturers are familiar with all the risks of total competition at continental level, including that of unpopularity. And from this position, they are also firmly entrenched worldwide, giving full support to the opening of global markets.

With its history and its pride, the automobile is an asset within the not-so-large number of European industries that excel at world level.

It does not take a long speech to demonstrate how important the good health of the European automobile industry is to that of the economy and society of Europe as a whole.

The added value of motor vehicles and motor vehicle parts and accessories account for 9% of the entire manufacturing industry, and almost 2% of the entire GDP of the European Union.

The direct employees amount to 1.8 million, or 8% of the total workforce employed by the manufacturing industry of the Union; but if we consider the whole system that rotates around the motor vehicle, we must add another 11 - 12 million people. This means almost 10% of the total working population.

The contribution to total exports outside the European Union remained high, at about 8-10%, throughout the eighties and the balance of trade shows a surplus, although this has been falling in recent years.

And the motor vehicle is an important source, sometimes even the leading source, of tax revenue for Member States. In 1992 over 200 billion ECU were accounted for by direct and indirect taxes on the purchase of cars, spare parts, repairs, car ownership and fuel.

Apart from economic factors, the enormous value of the automobile industry is also expressed in terms of technical impetus and spin-offs. From this point of view, the auto industry is an extremely powerful lever, which is effective on two levels.

The first, of an industrial nature, derives from intrinsic process and product specifications, which call for the application of a vast spectrum of technologies, demanding constant innovation inside and outside the industry.

The second level is tied to the enormous influence that the car has on society and, more specifically, the primary role that the transport system plays in contributing to the international competitiveness of a geographic area.

What the European economy and European citizens now want is a modern system for moving goods and people throughout the continent, at lower cost, appropriate speed, with personal safety and with the lowest environmental impact. Jacques Delors expressed this very well in his recent White Paper. In Europe, there is an enormous need to improve transport networks and traffic management systems, through a huge, lasting common commitment by public institutions at all levels, and private sector groups.

In this context, the automobile industry makes an enormous contribution to innovation with its safer, less polluting products, with telematics (of which we saw a concrete application in Brussels in January), with vehicle recycling operations, and with proposals for the solution of urban traffic problems.

It is clear that today the automobile industry can no longer be considered as merely the manufacturer of a product. It is also one of the players in the rationalisation and growth of the mobility system. In other words, a virtuous technological circle between manufacturing and consumption, the distinguishing element of a modern society, is in the process of evolving.

Industrial Restructuring

In the car sector, production methods and interaction with the market tend to evolve in much the same way in the three big regions of the world. Competitiveness is measured not only by the quality of products and services - the true challenge of the modern age, in a market where it is the consumer who sets the rules - but also by costs and reaction times.

The level of competition in the sector shows a constant growth in the number and types of market actors. This competition is particularly marked in Europe, where practically all the world's manufacturers operate. Given the size of our internal market, at the moment still the world's largest, all the manufacturers are aiming to improve their presence here.

Competition is not a new phenomenon for the industry.

The history of the European automobile reflects a constant striving after competitiveness, within the constraints and opportunities, initially of the national, and thereafter of the European, business environment. Normally, this goal can be achieved by improving existing factors, within each individual area of the company. But at a certain point, if the external context changes radically, either because something new occurs or because weaknesses that have developed over time accumulate to a critical point, this method is no longer enough. It takes radical action on all the structures of the company: in other words a breakthrough and not only constant improvement.

At the moment, Europe is right in the middle of one of these cycles. One had already occurred in the early eighties, and another is happening again, in a more radical, more complex and more expensive form today.

Today the European automobile industry cannot afford to merely align itself with the current state-of-the-art of the competition, because in the meantime it will not stand still. It is absolutely essential to take giant steps forward in terms of competitiveness and do even better than the improvements that are underway in other regions.

The challenge is therefore a double one. What is more, it is coming at a moment of acute market crisis.

So, the European automobile industry must at the same time:

- respond globally and quickly to the demands of the consumer and the population in general;

- lower the break-even point, increasing productivity in the company as a whole;

- increase flexibility in production and management.

All this implies radical changes in production methods in the factory, in company organisation, in relations with suppliers and dealers, in the professional qualifications of the workforce and, more generally, in the attitudes of Society itself.

To achieve these results, it is not enough to act strictly within the automobile industry. We must extend the restructuring process to the components industry and recreate the relationship between the two industries on new partnership foundations. We have to act on the variables outside the sphere of company management which influence and condition the sector's competitiveness.

There can be no doubt that the automobile industry itself has primary responsibility for the restructuring process. In fact it has already taken important steps on its own, and will continue to do so, at a fast rate.

Plant productivity has increased (in some cases by as much as 50% compared to the eighties); the manufacturing process is being thoroughly reorganised; product development times have been slashed; new relationships have been forged with components' suppliers; more efficient use is being made of information technology. A great deal has been invested in training: 20% more from 1989 to 1992.

Concrete co-operation between manufacturers in R&D has been envisioned, identifying the areas where research in common is both more important and more feasible:

-    vehicle development and manufacturing processes;

-    new technologies for emissions and fuel economy;

-    light vehicle structures and materials;.

-    electric/electronic components for electric/hybrid vehicles.

Restructuring activities frequently and necessarily entail personnel reductions, worsened by market conditions, which have a substantial effect given the size of the industry. These sometimes lead to new solutions in other industries too and therefore take on a symbolic nature, putting car manufacturers in the eye of the storm.

The Barriers to Restructuring

I have said that this process of transformation and growth requires a consistent external context. The European automotive industry has to tackle numerous barriers, which at best slow down progress and often require a change in the course of action.

There are different types of barriers.

The first one regards the sphere of cultures and attitudes.

Restructuring implies a radical change in traditional ways of producing, working, managing personnel, organisations and markets, and the capability to dominate change over time, with maximum flexibility. Unfortunately there is tremendous resistance in this field. A lack of co-ordination among all the players called on to make a contribution is a critical element. We hope that a strong commitment to work for change may emerge from this Forum, which includes representatives of institutions, companies and the Unions.

There is also considerable difficulty in understanding industrial logic. It is probable that the root of the problem lies with our schools. We should draw them closer to the worlds of industry and business.

We often observe paradoxical situations in the relationship between society and industry: the rhetoric of the post-industrial age but the continuing indispensable nature of industry; the revolt against consumer society but the defence of employment; efficiency and innovation but also the protection of what already exists; free trade ideology and the need to cope with its far-reaching social consequences.

Finally, there is the problem of communication, among all protagonists. We have to talk to each other more, within and among all the parties involved at the appropriate level; particularly at the local level, where problems are best understood and where effective decisions can be made.

The second type of barriers concerns political institutions.

It is absolutely necessary for the single European market to be completed as soon as possible.

As long as today's differences remain within the European Union, in terms of taxes and regulations, Europe will be impaired in its taking a strong stand against international competition. The lack of harmonisation of certain standards - particularly those regarding the environment - creates competitivity gaps even inside Europe itself.

To this we must add the tension between European countries on basic economic factors. One example will suffice. For many years up to 1992 average inflation in Italy was much higher than the European rate and the overvalued Lira, at a fixed exchange rate, created cost imbalances and anomalous behaviour. Suddenly, when the Lira was devalued at the end of 1992, the imbalances changed sign.

How can industry which plans and operates complex programmes and huge investments in the very long term, bear such an imposition? The single European currency is the ultimate goal which all efforts should be directed towards, in the best interest of European industry.

The possibility of incorporating a single European corporation, with a single taxation system, may perhaps appear Utopian today, but all of us are presently working in an environment which strongly requires ambitious vision.

Further, in backing efforts to change the automobile industry, the institutions must favour transparency and effective action.

More than in the past, today's restructuring, as I have said, may be expensive in social terms: intrinsically, and because it is taking place in a period of already serious unemployment and unfavourable conditions for investment.

So it becomes necessary to tackle the problem of the reduction in manpower together. The European Commission and national governments are called upon to set up the conditions needed to foster the creation of new jobs and to introduce programmes for worker retraining. The real challenge is not to protect existing jobs, even when they are no longer productive, but to create new ones.

The other important act, which is the prime responsibility of the European Commission, consists in undertaking initiatives which accompany the transformation of this sector. Without reopening the debate on sectoral policies versus horizontal policies, to ask for a "Policy for Industry" means to ask for an <u>integrated</u> approach on the part of the Commission. Research policies, trade policies, competition policies, social policies, environmental policies, and so on, must not be seen each in isolation but must all converge on the final goal of greater competitiveness for the European industrial system, respecting free competition but pragmatically bearing in mind the actual situation on the market.

Giving a few concrete examples, this could mean:

- favouring R&D joint initiatives, which are transferred from the realm of general research to that of application in innovative products and processes;

- avoiding the adoption of legislation which aggravates rigidity;

- carefully analysing costs-vs-benefits prior to issuing environmental regulations, which must be homogeneous and stable; on the contrary, some amendments proposed by the EP to the emissions Directive proposal are inconsistent with this approach, because they ignore the current state-of-the-art technology and have lost contact with the prevailing industrial and economic reality. They could have a negative impact on the credibility of the Commission itself if pursued without reconsideration;

- protecting the development and the investments the manufacturers are contributing to their own distribution system, in the interest of better service to their clients;

- protecting the outcome of intellectual activities performed by manufacturers, which devote long, painful and costly attention to internal skills and know-how;

- negotiations on effective free trade conditions with full reciprocity between different world regions.

We all know that different pressures and interests come into play in some of these subjects. The debate is open.

The third type of barrier is found in the world of labour.

Cultural and behavioural barriers of the type I mentioned earlier emerge in labour relations.

Resistance to change is still deeply rooted whereas flexibility should be the guiding light in the new course of the economy and European society.

Inside the company, for example, flexibility means:

- a few basic certainties and readiness to question everything else afresh;

- acceptance of mobility of function and role;

- readiness to delegate and assume responsibility;

- greater interaction and better integration.

Where the labour market is concerned, I think that the way in which Jacques Delors' White Paper expresses the concept of the improvement of external flexibility was very appropriate: putting a large number of unemployed in a position to meet the requirements identified by companies.

Another obstacle is the inadequacy of the basic education and vocational training system to meet the needs of industry and modern society.

We must expand the general knowledge base, with more focus on information science, mathematics, communication, and team-oriented and learning techniques. We must redirect vocational training courses towards a "multi-skill" approach which is essential for the new way of manufacturing.

Industry is trying to obviate the current inadequacies through its own vocational training initiatives, but these entail additional costs and in any case do not guarantee the same results that would be achieved if internal training were linked with a school system that is less tied to the past.

Then there are all the aspects related to labour costs.

We ask the government and trade unions of each country to help to reduce non-wage costs, frequently ineffective and inappropriate, and to continue the joint efforts which have recently been made towards more progressive systems of labour management.

All these barriers, which we could call structural, combine with an extremely negative cycle.

Market data reflect a recession such as Western Europe had not seen since the War.

1993 closed with a 15.9% fall in demand for cars and LCVs (up to 5t) which means 2 million fewer vehicles than in 1992. All European countries were affected, except the United Kingdom, which was already very weak before.

We cannot expect much improvement in the medium term. ACEA forecasts for 1994 indicate that the market for cars will remain substantially stationary (+ 1.1 %); a stronger improvement is expected for 1995 (+6%), but sales volumes will still fall 1,200,000 cars short of 1992 levels.

We are therefore faced with a more serious crisis than in the past, because it combines the intensity of the collapse of the first oil crisis with the duration of the crisis of the early eighties.

If we consider commercial vehicles, the situation is even worse.

In the last four years the European market has continuously fallen and in 1993 the slump was particularly strong: 347,000 vehicles (3.5 tonnes and above) were registered, 21.4% fewer than in 1992. In 1989 there were 510,000. Forecasts for 1994 point perhaps to a further reduction. If all goes well we will have to wait for 1995 to see a turn-around.

We must be aware that market cycles will be the rule for the future. All manufacturers must be able to adapt constantly.

This brings us to a final consideration.

All the work which is underway to restructure the automotive industry goes in parallel with, and in actuality is part of a major development programme which involves huge investments and - therefore - the deployment of huge capital.

The manufacturers must remain in a position to provide long-term self-finance, even through the slumps in market cycles.

The European automotive industry will continue to play its decisive role in terms of size and technology, also in the better interests of the European economy and welfare.

But it will no longer be in condition to act as a collector, a solver, a crucible of every kind of need which is not compatible with its competitiveness - this is because, if all the demands from all different sources were to be accepted, it would no longer be possible to generate resources for the future, and we would be correctly accused of badly managing our business.

We must be aware that this is not only a process of restructuring in the normal sense, but we are actually laying the foundations for the long-term future. This process cannot be seen as a more tactical answer to existing external pressure, but to a more strategic move on which our industry is committing a good part of its future development with far-reaching consequences for the whole of the European economy.

Thank you.

Mr Perissich:

Thank you Ing. Garuzzo. Monsieur Planchon please.

Mr Planchon:

Good Morning Ladies and Gentlemen.

Not so long ago, in the early Seventies, in addition to a handful of historically renowned suppliers, more than ten thousand small family-owned European automotive sub-contractors produced parts on the basis of drawings handed by vehicle manufacturers.

Today, some 3000 independent suppliers, with sales of nearly 100 Bn ECUs and employment of 940,000 in the European Union, provide parts and systems equal to at least 50 % of the production value of all European cars and trucks. CLEPA federates the efforts and interests of Europe's national associations of automotive component and system suppliers.

Ninety percent of these companies are SMEs employing less than 500 people (on average 300), while some 130 suppliers - 4 % of the total number - represent half of our industry's employment. The top 25 firms account for 55 % of industry sales.

Compared to the United States or Japan where a single factory would suffice to produce a particular part, the European supplier industry is still highly fragmented, reflecting Europe's national mosaic and the protection until recently given by all vehicle manufacturers to national suppliers. Ninety per cent of SMEs' sales are still local, and until recently 90 % of vehicle manufacturers' sourcing has been with national suppliers.

By the year 2000, the BCG forecasts no more than 500 First Tier System Suppliers operating in Europe, with remaining suppliers reduced by up to one third. For the most part, these would be producing components and sub-assemblies or supplying highly specialised or local services to First Tier System Suppliers.

In addition to this rationalisation, many suppliers have today several factories within the Union's borders, each producing quasi identical products - not because of economic considerations or client-related logistics, but because of history, customer sourcing preference, natural reluctance to confront legal rigidities for closure, or inability to fund massive shutdown costs. There are also new situations where suppliers have now to localise in order to help absorb excess manpower at customer locations.

European Supplier Industry Competitiveness

Over the last three years, European suppliers have been heavily engaged in implementing lean manufacturing programmes, achieving substantial improvements in productivity and quality through better involvement of people, flatter and more transparent structures, more efficient production processes and logistics, more (but still insufficient) involvement of second tier suppliers. We have become obsessed with crushing costs and with continuous improvement.

Our customers have less time, people and money to deal with increasingly specialised areas of technology. Mobilising and managing brain-power to achieve efficient project management, reliable speed and ever shorter development times has been a must. With our customers, we are working to make products more compact, lighter, noiseless, long-life, easy to assemble, user-friendly and recyclable. Technology has indeed become a key differentiator.

Investment in R&TD for leading firms exceeds on average 5 %, while another 7 to 8 % per annum is invested in new equipment and manufacturing processes. Training is another key ingredient of competitiveness. 5 % of payrolls is required annually to evolve the industrial culture of our enterprises, by raising the levels of technical competence and of quality, cost and customer awareness.

Many European suppliers have demonstrated their capacity to match the levels of performance of their best competitors world-wide. Many have been retained to serve the Euro-Japanese transplants and have learned a great deal from these relationships; nearly all have seen their contracts renewed for the next generation of models.

Having said this, our industry still must - and can - improve on many fronts in the pursuit of world-class performance. This is a race with no finish line and the pace at which we are progressing must now be significantly increased. With our customers we must compete in the global market, yet in many parts of the European Union we have to live with levels of industrial flexibility, working hours, machine utilisation rates and total labour costs which are not competitive.

Costs and practices must be geared to the global market place. This must be accomplished by harnessing the potential and creativity of our people - with the positive contribution of our social partners - to achieve more quality, productivity, innovation and growth. Our challenge is to achieve this in Europe - not by relocating Europe's supply base to far away lands.

But together we must face the truth: in the end, in a global market, market forces always win - ultimately they dictate industrial strategy and public policy.

Ladies and Gentlemen, we want Europe to win!

Public Policy and Competitive Conditions - Barriers, Handicaps and Reciprocity

Only six years remain to bring the structural change relating to our industry to a successful conclusion. The car models of year 2000 will be finalised in two years' time!

The Commission and national governments must ensure that balanced competitive conditions - a level playing field - prevail in the European Union.

Restructuring

The European supplier industry faces over-capacity, industrial mutation and heavy restructuring costs. The initiative for meeting these challenges lies in the hands of individual companies; however, the cost of shedding the structures imposed by 50 years of European social and political history should be shouldered by long-term, low-cost, Community financing. This should be the first pillar of the "volet interne", in particular for the SMEs. Suppliers should be able to concentrate their funds to support the new and increasing role demanded by their customers and by European consumers.

Today, European Member States and regions financially assist the establishment by non-European suppliers of green-field manufacturing sites in Europe. As a priority, the Commission should ensure that sectorial support is provided first to European companies, transforming their enterprises to meet world-class benchmarks, lest European taxpayers be made to ultimately pay twice the price!

R&TD

The Commission has acknowledged the essential need to support the industry's R&TD effort. The delayed final approval of the 4th Framework Programme is unfortunate in view of the critical timing for designing 2000-year vehicle models.

As currently defined, the programme does not allow relevant manufacturing process technologies to be included within the scope of each project - yet this is a key area where we need to progress toward world-class benchmarks.

Generally, the amount of support envisaged does not take sufficiently into account the broad spectrum of technologies relating to our industry, nor will it cover a sufficient share of the investment required to meet the environmental, safety, recycling and fuel economy challenges ahead. May I draw your attention in this regard to the transfer of important R&TD resources from military to automotive programmes in the United States.

We urge the Commission to increase the frequency of application for grants, to reduce time-consuming formalities, to consider projects of particular interest to our industry even if not falling precisely under one of the programme headings, and to give priority to proposals involving a strong OEM-Supplier link, thus contributing to strengthening the partnership concept. Moreover, allowing for the diversity in company size within our industry, minimum project amounts should be at accessible levels for SME projects.

To make real progress within the short timeframe available, programmes would gain from being more flexible, more accessible and more sectorially-oriented.

Education and Training

Industry needs and talks about teamwork while the educational system still promotes elitism and individual success, which remain in the forefront of our social and business reward system. How can industry and public policy afford to be in such contradiction? Industry loses precious time and money in reorienting incoming personnel.

We do not agree with the Commission's Communication when it suggests that "human resources, adequate training and motivation are key factors in industrial competitiveness once levels of mechanisation and automation are attained.." Quite the contrary: first and foremost, we must break down the mindset of people at all levels. This is key to changing our industrial culture and meeting the competitive challenges I have outlined.

We require strongly focused and easy access initial training and retraining programmes of pragmatic and immediate practical benefit.

Harmonisation and Industrial Concentration

We would like to encourage the Commission and the Member States to hasten completion of the internal market legal, tax and regulatory harmonisation processes. These are particularly costly to our industry, in particular to SMEs as they become increasingly Europe-wide in scope.

Also, mergers, acquisitions and other forms of inter-company co-operation should be viewed from a broader and more global standpoint by the Commission.

External Trade Policy

The future of the European components industry cannot be based on protectionism, but on global competitiveness. Within Europe, however, the same set of rules should apply to all. We need an effective External Trade Policy which deals expeditiously against dumping practices, the sale of pirate parts, chronic unbalanced trade resulting from closed market situations.

The 1991 Europe-Japan understandings totally ignored the European components industry, while the 1992/93 US-Japan agreements created a $19bn sales opportunity for American components - roughly 25 % of which was in exports to Japan!

In 1992, exports of Japanese automotive components into the European Union were already five times the level of European component exports to Japan, and the US-Japan agreement can only impact negatively on any opportunity which European suppliers might have to export to Japan. Volume is key to global competitivity, and reciprocity for our industry with Japan should become a prime objective of the Commission in 1994.

European suppliers can and must satisfy Euro-Japanese vehicle manufacturers with the agreed levels of European local content in qualitative, quantitative and competitive terms, thereby ensuring they buy in Europe and do not create further excess-capacity through the introduction of additional Japanese component transplants. The American experience in this connection cannot be ignored.

During the coming five years, the flow of trade with the newly emerging automotive producing countries will also need to be carefully monitored and balanced. Extremely low salaries and the virtual absence of social welfare costs will significantly impact on the European market, if uncontrolled. Reciprocity arrangements will need to be considered.

Industry Solidarity - Winning Together in Europe and Worldwide

Domestic Markets provide Critical Mass and Systems Sponsorship

In both North America and Japan, the leading vehicle manufacturers have developed their own component subsidiaries, whose sales in 1992 only for their eight principal entities exceeded 60bn ECUs - two-thirds the size of the entire European supply industry. While these affiliates are established or expanding their activities in Europe, it has been virtually impossible so far for European suppliers to sell competing products to their parent companies in their domestic market.

World competitiveness requires critical mass in addition to technological and manufacturing excellence. We must be able to compete with reciprocity on level playing fields.

Symbiosis in Europe

We believe it is in the long-term-self-interest of European vehicle manufacturers to be able to rely on a strongly competitive, healthy and independent European supplier base.

CLEPA member companies are totally committed to this objective. Also they require the strategic support of European vehicle manufacturers to achieve critical mass and maintain technological and systems leadership capability in Europe.

Competitive prices are a must; however, reinforced solidarity and strategic considerations are also needed in day-to-day industry decisions.

Partnership relations at Tier One level are evolving rapidly, but they are nevertheless still insufficient, not early enough, often duplicatory and still laden with suspicion on both sides. Suppliers must improve their reliability score to overcome these situations. The customer is King!

With downstream suppliers, the development of true partnership relations, essential to achieve industry cost competitiveness at a profit, has only now begun. Acceptance of the need to act rapidly on costs, quality and attitude has generally been too slow at Tier Two level - certainly not in line with vehicle manufacturers' demands to reduce system costs by 20 to 25 % from one vehicle generation to the next within the next two years.

Mutual Benefits from the Aftermarket

Both vehicle and component manufacturers should recognise and respect each other's significant interests in the aftermarket. There will always be an independent aftermarket and forbidding its access to component manufacturers only results in greater proliferation of sub-standard, non-type-approved, pirate parts. We should pursue counterfeit products jointly, and examine with the Commission how to deal with the tidal wave of imports to be expected during the second half of the nineties from new automotive-producing countries.

Becoming more Global

Many of us have already migrated with our customers East and West, mustering the necessary talents and resources to operate at their side.

Automotive industry growth in China, Korea, Southeast Asia, India, Turkey, Eastern Europe, Mexico and South America underscores the need to pursue a more global European presence - equal at least to that of our American and Japanese competitors. Within the next ten years, these markets will produce as many vehicles as Europe, Japan or the United States. Consider the economic impact of such volume on vehicle and component costs!

We must be present alongside our customers in this global development strategy. The Commission should organise the necessary European educational, medical and cross-cultural social facilities and make long-term financing facilities available to support individual projects, as is done for our major international competitors.

Conclusion

Ladies and Gentlemen, there is no longer room nor time for adversarial relationships or energy-consuming procedures. We must all move to "win-win" modes. Our fate as suppliers depends on each of our customers' capacity to survive and prosper; conversely, we play a decisive role in shaping our customers' competitive position.

Let's be sure to "win together" within the next 3 years - well before 1999.

Thank you for your attention and support.

Mr Perissich:

Thank you Mr Planchon. I would like to remind the speakers that unless they do keep to the suggested time limits, there will not only not be time for the question and answer session, but there won't even be time for all the speakers to speak.

Mr Jordan, please.

Mr Jordan:

Thank you Chairman. I'm used to them changing the rules when it gets to my turn!

The automobile industry is probably the most competitive industry in the world, and the way in which Europe tackles the challenge that that competition presents will indicate the likely outcome in the wider battle for supremacy that is shaping up among the world's three leading trading blocks. Europe's political power must be in the driving seat when the policies are made if we are to determine a successful outcome to that battle. The future competitiveness of Europe's industries cannot be left entirely to the globetrotting, profit-chasing whims of the multinationals. Partners - yes, but on terms that leave some protection for Europe's workers when the multinationals' capital goes walkabout.

Why is the auto industry such an important testbed? The truth is that Europe has not been doing well in the world's manufacturing race. An OECD study of thirteen leading industrialised countries calculates that in the past twenty years manufacturing employment has fallen by 8 %, but in Europe it has fallen by 20 %, while in the USA it has hardly changed, and in Japan it has risen, by 2 %.

Coming from a country that has seen its manufacturing workforce drop from 7 million to 4 million in just over a decade, and has seen its own only British-owned volume car maker being sold off to BMW a few weeks ago, I have had reason to think long and hard about those factors I have seen at work in world-class manufacturing. I have had cause to curse the politically driven ideological experimentation that has wrought such havoc in the UK's manufacturing capacity.

Europe is the world's largest car market and the world's largest producer, but we do need to remind ourselves that 30 % of our production is foreign-owned.

America, on the back of a radical development in car manufacturing in the first part of the century, colonised the industrial world with its car making facilities.

The last twenty years has seen the Japanese coming like manufacturing missionaries, setting up their automotive missions in Europe and even in the shadow of the temples of the USA's "Big Three" car producers.

It's a history of new ideas ousting old, and Europe following, where others have led. It does not have to be like that, but first we have to master the new ideas, and hold the ground we have - a job we're not doing well, a job the Commission can, and must, play a part in.

I worry when I hear the word "restructuring". Too often in Europe it has been used as a signal for a disorderly retreat in the face of competition, and I warn this audience that unless we have policies that entrench the ingredients of world-class manufacturing into Europe's auto industry, any restructuring will simply be a programme of decline.

There are acknowledged ingredients in world-class manufacturing. Amongst them is sustained investment in new technology, in research and development, and in design and marketing. All of these are vital, and with these factors, you get what you are prepared to pay for.

However, the essence of the new manufacturing techniques - lean production, or whatever word you want to use - is people power. At its best, and I've seen it at its best and been a part of it, it is a partnership between employers, Union and employees. It is a partnership that embraces a commitment from all concerned to work for the aspirations of each of the partners. For employers, it brings the benefit of Union and employee support for a kaleidoscope of techniques and practices that, taken together, are capable of unleashing a phenomenal performance improvement embracing both productivity and quality. For Unions and their members, it brings a degree of openness, truthfulness and two-way communication that is rare in European industry. Single-status employment that brings with it common conditions; a level of training that embraces every employee in a career development policy, and a commitment to a degree of job security that a majority of European employers find unacceptable. How is it that so many of Europe's employers know each of these ingredients so well, and yet that so many find it difficult to bring them together under one roof?

What can the Commission do to help improve the levels of competitiveness in Europe's auto industry? It cannot command change. It can, and should, promote best practice. But I would prefer to see the efforts and resources of the Commission going into three factors, which more than most would help industry deal effectively with the continual change and intensifying competition that Europe will continue to face. Those factors are training, job security and social partnership.

The fact is that the automotive industry of the twenty-first century will not require unskilled or semi-skilled workers, and unless European policies, education and training policies are geared to that fact, we will be on a loser. Commission money can help to create a training infrastructure, but to meet the size of the present challenge, vocational training in Europe must be made as compulsory as education. Europe-wide minimum training targets must be set, and if they are to be met, training must be a rate that every employee can claim. The message to every employer must be "Train or pay a levy". Stealing the skills that others train cannot be an option in a world-class Europe. Europe's Trade Unions do not expect employment for life for their members, but we do demand a level and a continuity of training for skills that will give our members employability for life.

Rover Cars, not all that long ago, symbolised what we call "The British Disease". Now its dramatic transformation has made it the sort of company most UK companies would like to be - a partnership of company, unions and employees, and the radical change that they have achieved was made possible by the foundation stone of job security underpinning it. It's a job security concept composed of two elements: a guarantee of no compulsory redundancies, and a willingness to fund voluntary redundancy and early retirement.

The first is a must for any company that is serious about being world class. It's not an absolute commitment to jobs for life, but the practice of demonstrating to a workforce that whatever difficulties the companies face, the very last solution is going to be the loss of the employees' jobs. The Commission should provide funds that facilitate early retirement in such restructuring packages, but it must be made a condition of payment that a guarantee of no compulsory redundancies be in company agreements.

How do we get a partnership? You cannot legislate for people to co-operate. In Europe's best companies, employees and Unions do co-operate, but in Europe's auto industry, and in its wider manufacturing industry, its best companies are not the problem. It's not the best assemblers and component makers in this room or on this platform, it's the vast underclass of low performing companies that grab our average performance down. It's the thousands and thousands of companies where there is no dialogue, social or otherwise.

We have to make European best practice, standard practice; give every European employee the right to representation and the right to be heard at the place of work. For the employer, the duty to inform, through representation, a workforce entitled to know of matters affecting their livelihood. A chance to bring forth the wealth of ideas and experience that lies for the most part unused in our industries. It is beyond belief that employers whose future depends on making changes are resisting the draft directive on Multinational Works Councils. Could there be a better platform from which to preach company-wide best practice? But the same Council that talks of better productivity, equality and profits, must also talk of better working conditions, health and safety and job security for those who will deliver the improved performance. The Commission could help to break down the irrational resistance of the employers by making known the success of European Works Council agreements between the European Metalworkers' Federation and some of Europe's major multinationals, including the automotive industry.

Across a wider front, the Commission can and must help in a thousand ways in Europe's long march to competitiveness. The Commission, employers and Unions must be prepared to embrace radical change if we are to create a real partnership. Teamworking at national level between the Social Partners can be as effective as we've seen it on the shopfloor of the automotive industry.

Protectionism is a short-term solution. You cannot build a wall high enough or strong enough that will keep out the forces of change. Partnership is a difficult path, but a more certain one to European competitiveness. Europe's Trade Unions are prepared to read that path, but only as equal partners, not as silent ones.

Thank you.

Mr Perissich:

Thank you Mr Jordan. You have also proved that one can say a hell of a lot of things in ten minutes!

We have heard the views, authoritatively expressed, on the restructuring of the car industry from the representatives of the key actors. I now go on to the Panel. Unfortunately Mr Sainjon MEP is not here. The other members of the Panel are: Mr I. McAllister, Chairman, Ford of Britain, Mr P. Lepoutre, President of CECRA, the European Committee for Motor Trades and Repairs, and Mr H. Neumann of the German IG-Metall Trade Union. They are to comment on the exposés that we have been listening to.

Mr McAllister, please.

Mr McAllister:

Thank you. Let me start by giving a commercial. Mr Garuzzo said that Industry has got to deal with the problems of restructuring themselves, and I think that Industry recognises that and is getting on with the job. Substantial progress has been made across Europe in the past few years in terms of improving our productivity. Speaking for Ford and speaking for Britain, our productivity has improved by over 40 % since 1990, and we are closing the gap that has traditionally existed between our British plants and our continental plants. Our objective is to meet and to beat the anticipated productivity of the Japanese by 1997, and I know how productive they are, because they're all in my back yard!

Enough of the commercial. Let me deal with some of the issues, and some of the barriers to restructuring that I've noticed today. Herr Bangemann spoke about the importance of innovation, and Mr Planchon mentioned that technology is the key to differentiation.

I feel very uncertain about some of these issues because we perceive a major threat to our technological base from the assembly facilities that have been set up in the EU by manufacturers from the Far East. These manufacturers are assembling vehicles which have been designed and engineered overseas, and all those high value-added, high wage, highly skilled jobs associated with the design and engineering of those vehicles are in the Far East. Increases in such sales within Europe will hollow out our European skills base, and will reduce our long-term capability to compete.

So the issue for the industry is, I think, how to retain the skills within Europe to ensure a long-term viable industry. To do that we have to nurture the research and development capability that we have. We certainly have plenty of engineers. One of the problems is, however, that the structure of the European Union's research and development funds makes it difficult for us to use those funds effectively, because the Union insists on making the provision of those funds on a horizontal basis across industry. I think that if we are serious in improving the technological capability of our industry, we should look at focusing those research and technological development funds specifically at issues within the automobile industry.

The second issue which Herr Bangemann touched on was the importance of completing the internal market, and I would like to address the importance of vehicle regulations to the automotive industry. None of us is objecting to cars that are safe, nor to cars that are environmentally friendly, but for us to use our resources efficiently, the regulations must be set as early as possible so that our engineers can work towards them. The last thing we can deal with efficiently is a change in regulations, and that's why we would certainly strongly recommend that there should be no changes in the planned emissions regulations for 1996, simply because they would be late, and any change is inefficient in terms of our usage of engineers, and would also reduce quality.

If the industry wishes to compete efficiently on a global basis, then I would recommend that the Commission looks at harmonising European standards with the standards in the rest of the world, because it is far more efficient for us to engineer our vehicles to compete on a global basis than to have to engineer them to compete in individual sectors of the world.

The final issue I would like to talk about very quickly is the distribution system for vehicles in Europe. The whole issue of block exemption is coming up for renewal, we all know that. We believe that Europe is fully competitive in that sense, and we are concerned that any change will have significant consequences on unemployment within the distribution trade. It would be a very significant shift for them.

Perhaps most importantly, the industry is going through the most serious restructuring process of the last fifty years, and this at a time of major recession in Europe. The last thing that we would like to see as manufacturers is the diversion of our efforts to dealing with a fundamental shift in the distribution structure. We believe that we should be concentrating on improving competitiveness, not having to discuss the investment issues, in my case of 900 separate independent traders, in order to help them through a problem that has been created by a shift in distribution which isn't required, and in my view, frankly, isn't needed either.

Thank you Mr Perissich.

Mr Perissich:

Thank you Mr McAllister. Monsieur Lepoutre.

📕 *Mr Lepoutre:*

Thank you Mr Chairman.

In the name of CECRA, which is the European Committee for Motor Trades and Repairs, I am very happy to be here and to be able to continue on some of the issues raised by my predecessors, namely that of distribution.

Before that, I would like to make some points on the importance of the distribution network, which, I would remind you, is represented here by CECRA, in the name of seventeen national member associations of the CECRA, comprising the twelve Member States of the Union.

250,000,000 companies, SMEs;

2,000,000 employees;

Several categories of enterprises;

- official networks, concessionary agents;

- independent enterprises, with no brand name;

- specialised companies, working in a particular sector.

It is clear that the brand-owned networks occupy the most important position as regards the sale of brand new cars: 100,000 companies, employing some 1,100,000 people. The size of the companies in the distribution network varies according to a series of criteria - urban, rural, etc. Whatever the size, it is always an independent company, with their own capital invested in the brand name, and responsible for the jobs they have created. These companies are controlled within a legal framework known as "selective and exclusive distribution", organised by the Union, by Exemption Regulation 123/85.

What are the main characteristics, very briefly, of an economic group which achieves the feeding into the market of manufactured vehicles, and the use of the product by the consumer? These companies have to meet many significant challenges:

- the need to change because of reduction in profit margins;

- the need to increase investment;

- training;

- new consumer attitudes;

- increased competition;

- brand mergers;

- concerns over the future of the system.

These challenges mean that the distribution company, to remain competitive in the market, broadens out from new cars to second-hand cars, spares, repair workshops, etc.

Increased competition has led the consumer to increased requirements, a significant challenge to distributors, because the consumer is much less faithful to a brand than in the past. The quality/price relationship has become less important than brand image in the consumer's eyes.

Offering good services at competitive prices will be henceforward the principle way to keep customers, and this can only be done by a company with appropriate buildings, efficient workshops, modern equipment, and qualified personnel.

Is the distribution system up to these challenges? We think it is. Distribution companies must change to face the new competitive, technological, consumer and social realities. Some might call this lean distribution.

There must be real co-operation between manufacturer and distributor: co-operation based on economic partnership, with reciprocal trust and a will to participate. Economic success requires the making of these relationships.

The selective and exclusive distribution network has been the sole manner in which new cars have been sold in the world and in the Union for seventy years, and it must be maintained. Seventy years of success must show the way for the next seventy years. Exemption Regulation 123/85 is based on a balance between the interests of the manufacturer, the distributors and the consumer.

CECRA believes that the reasoning that led the Commission to issue the Regulation eight years ago is still appropriate today. Second-hand cars are durable goods, and this necessitates close co-operation between the manufacturer and the distributor, a vital link which must be maintained.

A decision should be taken fast, so that the heads of the distributing companies are confident of their future, and will invest.

Thank you.

Mr Perissich:

Thank you Mr Lepoutre. And now Mr Neumann from the German IG-Metall.

📖 ***Mr Neumann:***

Thank you. I should like to make three comments.

First and foremost, the automobile industry is going through a dramatic change. It was certainly a good idea to have a conference along these lines today. We've been wanting one for ages. I say this as a member of the IG-Metall Trade Union. We feel that the Commission paper represents considerable progress from what has been done so far.

Perhaps I could just correct one point, however. This is one of the biggest industries in Europe. 1.8 million employees has been mentioned in the document. Mr Garuzzo has mentioned this. Others have talked about 11 million. In Germany, 1.5 million people are involved in production, so I suppose there must be 4-5 million in Europe as a whole. It is of great importance not to lose sight of the fact that we are talking here of such a huge number of people, 4-5 million.

Second point: Both Mr Bangeman and the President of ACEA have said that there is one thing that is essential to us, and that it is competitiveness. This is not going to be achieved if we take on the role of accountants. I'm not saying that costs are not important, but we can only be profitable, as the White Paper says, if we follow a vision. We have to change our attitude; we must have a vision for the European automobile industry. There are three things we must do:

-   The environmental motor car must be developed. We don't want to have an alibi here, we want a three-litre motor car as fast as possible.

-   Vehicles must be produced in conditions which are humane for the employees. We know that this is not the case in Japan. Long working hours and low wages are very often the case. These cars are then sold cheaply in the US and in Europe. Human dignity is an important component of our challenge.

-   A reasonable price - DM 15,000 would be the sort of price we should be talking about for the mid-range car.

To do this by the end of the century, we are really going to have to move fast. We are going to have to change things to get ready to tackle such innovations - and this means changes in working hours and wages.

I don't think we can be reproached for being inflexible. I do feel that we should institutionalise this conference, so that we can forge an industrial policy, as Mr Jordan has said. New relationships have to be fostered, in which the Trade Unions are not seen as junior partners.

My third point is that we can be optimistic about the future of the automobile industry, if a few major challenges are taken up. There are five which I should like to pinpoint:

(i)   Overcapacity. I think this is a key word. I feel that a solution is vital to our competition with Japan. The opening up of the Japanese market is vital.

(ii) Co-operative supply contracts.

(iii) Further co-operation in innovation is also required. This has been well described in the Commission paper, and this must be encouraged.

(iv) Employment policy. We don't want to abandon this. Mr Bangemann talked about 100,000 jobs being lost. I don't think that's anything like a big enough figure. IG-Metall has talked about 150,000 jobs being lost unless we have the right sort of industrial policy, and I see this as being the main failure in the Commission's Communication: they haven't talked about a reduction in working hours. All sorts of different models have been applied. Flexibility is a vital concept here. Volkswagen can demonstrate this.

(v) Company management reform. Broader qualifications, a broader range of responsibilities. Mr Jordan talked about the power lying with human beings. Mr Bangemann has said that efficient work organisation is vital to enhanced competitiveness. Innovation in approaches to working hours, and last but not least, when you have hierarchical structures, and you talk about co-operation, then you are talking about the current phenomenon.

Thank you.

Mr Perissich:

Thank you Mr Neumann.

We have a little time left for a few questions. I have received some of them in a written form. Some of them I will pass on to the following moderator, but I would like to start this panel with a question from Mr Neal MacCall, co-ordinator of the Inter-Group for Automobile Users. If Mr MacCall is within reach of a microphone, he can formulate his qustion himself.

⚲ *Mr MacCall:*

Doesn't the Panel think that, in striving for a competitive edge, the industry shouldn't lose sight of the importance of vehicle safety?

Mr Perissich:

It's a pertinent question, and perhaps one for Mr Garuzzo and Mr Planchon.

⚲ *Mr Garuzzo:*

The answer is very simple: definitely "Yes". All the manufacturers believe that the improvement in safety both active and passive and the improvement in road safety is a must, a top priority, and in actuality a lot of our R&D budgets are devoted to such a task, and, in the past few years, everybody has seen improvements in our products in both in terms of active and passive safety.

At this stage I have answered the question, but I should like to just mention a problem which all this leaves on the shoulders of the car manufacturers. Given the need for increased safety, given the need for the protection of the environment, and given the need to develop new products, the R&D costs in our companies have skyrocketed. We are all now spending a lot of money. Nothing bad about that; as Mr McAllister has observed, this money goes into the more interesting part of our economy because it's money invested in research, in many different and related fields. The problem is we have to fund that R&D. For that reason, we believe that if there is an excess of competition, if the competition goes wild because of overcapacity, and manufacturers cannot find the necessary sums, this may in the end even harm the consumers - since any lack of funding for R&D is extremely damaging in this respect.

Thank you.

Mr Perissich:

Thank you very much. We still have a number of questions, and only time for one. Mr Julien Juillard, regional president of the CGC Trade Union in Peugeot Autombiles at Sochaux.

Mr Juillard:

I have listened with great attention to Mr Neumann and to Mr Jordan, and to the other speakers, who have all spoken on the major problems which the automobile industry will face in the future, on the social partnership, the importance of the Trade Unions and the changing employment infrastructures in the automobile sector. You have correctly pointed out that in the transplants there are a lot of young employees. The average age of those employed in a transplant is 28 - in other enterprises in Europe this is not the case. I listened to Mr Jordan who proposed the implementation of European funds to finance early retirement. In the various European countries there is a legal system for social protection which is in the throes of being implemented. I would simply like to ask the Panel what the resources are that the Union is able to give to the European manufacturing industry to help it face the restructuring challenge, to take measures regarding the age of employees, and to improve social protection and employment?

Mr Perissich:

I wonder whether an industry or a Trade Union representative on the Panel would like to answer this question. Mr Jordan?

Mr Jordan:

I've already made the point that the Commission can help industry with its problems but it can't solve those problems for it.

On the question of employment, all the contributions indicate that the changes that are with us and are to come will reduce the level of employment, particularly in the motor industry, and possibly that this will be reflected in the wider manufacturing industry, in any case, however efficient we get; but our challenge certainly in the Trade Unions is not that not a single job should be lost, but that not a single job should be lost needlessly; that what jobs will be going will go to the most competitive in the world. I've addressed and others have addressed those factors which undermine Europe's competitiveness and I've homed in on those three things, because you can tinker about with all these problems for ever and a day, you can talk about employers getting a new relationship with their employees - they've had 70 years to do this of their own volition - a minority of the best have. We have to make best practice standard practice, as I have said, and for that you need a few well-worded directives, to get the others off their backsides to face up to the competitive challenge that only a few of Europe's world-class companies are doing. You cannot wait for the voluntary approach to get you there, and I speak with bitter experience of what the voluntary approach has done to Britain's manufacturing industry, to its capacity and to its workforce. There have to be guidelines, there have to be targets, there has to be, as my colleague Neumann has said, vision. Without that, you will continue to trail behind those that lead the world in the new manufacturing techniques.

Mr Perissich:

Thank you. If no industry members of the panels wish to add anything .... then we have reached the end of the session. I should like to thank the members of the Panel for their contributions. We now have break for coffee, and the Forum will reconvene at 11.15 sharp. Thank you for your attention, ladies and gentlemen.

WORKSHOP 1

SUMMARY REPORT

MR R. PERISSICH
DIRECTOR GENERAL FOR INDUSTRY,
EUROPEAN COMMISSION

This workshop focused on the barriers to restructuring in the car industry of the European Union, and set the scene for the Forum as a whole, providing the background against which the other workshops elaborated on more operational issues. The principal speakers in this Workshop were the most senior from each grouping - the Presidents of the European automobile manufacturers' association, the European component manufacturers' association, and the European Metalworkers' Federation.

Each of these main speakers set out their view of the current situation of the European automobile industry, from the perspective of those they represent.

The Economic Importance of the Industry

Mr Garuzzo, President of the ACEA, pointed out how important the good health of the European automobile industry is to that of the economy and society of Europe as a whole: the motor vehicle is an important source, sometimes even the leading source, of tax revenue for Member States. He said the European automobile industry is soundly placed in the worldwide context and reaffirmed the European car manufacturers' full support for the opening of global markets.

Agreeing with President Delors' recent White Paper, he spelt out the enormous need to improve transport networks and traffic management systems through a huge, lasting common commitment by public institutions at all levels, and private sector groups. In this context, the European automobile industry makes an enormous contribution to innovation with its safer, less polluting products, with telematics, with vehicle recycling operations, and with proposals for the solution of urban traffic problems.

Mr Planchon, as President of the CLEPA, spoke for the motor vehicle component manufacturers. This sector comprises some 3000 independent suppliers, with sales of nearly ECU 100 Bn, and employs 940,000 people in the European Union. The component manufacturers provide parts and systems equal to at least 50 % of the production value of all European cars and trucks. Ninety percent of these companies are SMEs employing less than 500 people.

The European supplier industry is still highly fragmented. In Mr Planchon's view this is not because of economic considerations or client-related logistics, but because of history, customer sourcing preferences, or the inability to fund massive shutdown costs.

Mr Planchon also brought up how many European suppliers serve the Japanese transplants, and have learned a great deal from these relationships.

Mr Planchon described the mutual dependency of the component suppliers and the motor vehicle producers thus: "Our fate as suppliers depends on each of our customers' capacity to survive and prosper; conversely, we play a decisive role in shaping our customers' competitive position."

Mr Bill Jordan, CBE, is the President of the European Metalworkers' Federation, to which most of the Trade Unions in the automobile industry in Europe are affiliated. He concurred with the previous speakers on the importance and competitiveness of the automobile industry, adding that, "The way in which Europe tackles the challenge that that competition presents will indicate the likely outcome in the wider battle for supremacy that is shaping up among the world's three leading trading blocks. Europe's political power must be in the driving seat when the policies are made if we are to determine a successful outcome to that battle. The future competitiveness of Europe's industries cannot be left entirely to the globetrotting, profit-chasing whims of the multinationals. Partners - yes, but on terms that leave some protection for Europe's workers when the multinationals' capital goes walkabout."

Restructuring

For the producers, the challenge is to respond globally and quickly to the demands of the consumer, to lower the break-even point, increasing productivity still further, and to increase flexibility in production and management. Mr Garuzzo added that "All this implies radical changes in production methods in the factory, in company organisation, in relations with suppliers and dealers, in the professional qualifications of the workforce and, more generally, in the attitudes of Society itself. The automobile industry itself has primary responsibility for the restructuring process."

The barriers to restructuring are many and varied. Resistance to the radical changes that the need to restructure during the present recession requires has been met in "culture and attitudinal" spheres. Changes towards maximum flexibility are being made to the traditional ways of producing, working, and managing personnel. "We must be aware that this is not only a process of restructuring in the normal sense, but we are actually laying the foundations for the long-term future," Mr Garuzzo said.

For the Trade Unions, both Mr Jordan and Mr Neumann raised their concern that the restructuring process, if left completely in the hands of the management, would be "a programme of decline," particularly as regards the level of employment in the industry.

The restructuring challenge, in the view of Mr Neumann, lies in solving the problem of overcapacity, setting up co-operative supply contracts, fostering co-operation in innovation and bringing about changes in employment policy.

For Mr Neumann, we have to follow a vision with three components: the successful production and marketing of an environmental car ("We aren't looking for an alibi here - we want a three-litre motor car as fast as possible"); humane working conditions, and reasonable prices. To realise this vision, there may have to be changes in working hours and wages. Mr Neumann criticised the recent Communication from the Commission on the European Automobile Industry for not mentioning the "vital concept" of flexible working hours.

The requirement for restructuring in the automobile industry has been brought about, at least in part, by the proliferation of new manufacturing techniques. Mr Jordan said that the essence of lean production is "People power, a partnership between employers, Union and employees ... a commitment from all concerned ... a degree of openness, truthfulness and two-way communication ... a level of training that embraces every employee in a career development policy, and a commitment to a degree of job security."

Employment

The Forum took place a matter of weeks after Rover was taken over by BMW. Mr Jordan cited Rover as an example of successful Social Partnership. A promise of job security had underpinned the radical changes which had been undertaken by this company in recent years: "A guarantee of no compulsory redundancies, and a willingness to fund voluntary redundancy and early retirement ... whatever difficulties the companies face, the very last solution is going to be the loss of the employees' jobs ... Not that not a single job should be lost, but that not a single job should be lost needlessly."

Mr Jordan went on, "We have to make European best practice, standard practice. The fact is that the automotive industry of the twenty-first century will not require unskilled or semi-skilled workers, and unless European policies, education and training policies are geared to that fact, we will be on a loser. Commission money can help to create a training infrastructure, but to meet the size of the present challenge, vocational training in Europe must be made as compulsory as education. Stealing the skills that others train cannot be an option in a world-class Europe. Europe's Trade Unions do not expect employment for life for their members, but we do demand a level and a continuity of training for skills that will give our members employability for life."

On the issue of training, Mr Garuzzo felt the basic education and vocational training system in Europe is inadequate to meet the needs of industry and modern society. Vocational training courses should be directed towards a "multi-skill" approach, in his view.

Mr McAllister raised the training and retraining issue in the context of transplants, which pose a threat to the technological base in Europe by assembling vehicles which have been designed and engineered in the Far East, thus undermining the European skills base and reducing our long-term capability to compete.

The car manufacturers, according to Mr Garuzzo, find the Unions insufficiently flexible, however, and not prepared to accept mobility of function and role. He would also like to see different forms of contracts, enabling the manufacturers to reduce non-wage labour costs.

All the speakers agreed that restructuring would result in a significant decrease in the level of employment in the industry, and that there are important roles for the European Commission and national and regional authorities to play, in the spheres of training and retraining, the funding of early retirement and redundancy packages, and most importantly of all, in the creation of new jobs in other sectors.

Most of the speakers at the Forum would prefer to see the Commission's initiatives applied by sector, to ease access to these funds for any particular sector. Mr Garuzzo spelt out the measures he felt the EC should be taking to ease the transformation in the sector. These included favouring R&D joint initiatives, carefully analysing costs-vs-benefits as regards environmental regulations, which must be homogeneous and stable, and protecting the development and the investments the manufacturers are contributing to their own distribution system.

Regulation 123/85

The debate over the selective and exclusive distribution of motor vehicles (Regulation 123/85) on the European market was also raised in this Workshop.

Mr P. Lepoutre, President of CECRA, the European Committee for Motor Trades and Repairs, sat on the Panel of Workshop 1. Mr Lepoutre's argument for maintaining the exemption and retaining the system of selective distribution was that it reflected the way in which cars had been distributed in Europe throughout the seventy year history of the automobile market. In his view, the current Regulation provides a legal framework for a system balancing the interests of manufacturers, distributors and consumers, and CECRA believes that the reasoning that led the Commission to issue the Regulation eight years ago is still appropriate today.

Mr McAllister, the Chairman of Ford of Britain, also spoke about the selective distribution system. He was also in favour of prolonging the Block Exemption. To open the market for cars in Europe would change the distribution trade radically, would create unemployment and would divert the efforts of the manufacturers away from dealing with their more immediate restructuring challenges. They would be forced to cope with a fundamental shift in the distribution structure, moving to a completely free market from one which, in Mr McAllister's view, is already "fully competitive" - and all of this during the most serious recession and slump in demand since the war.

The Single Market

All the parties concerned in the Forum agreed that it is absolutely necessary for the single European market to be completed as soon as possible. The differences which remain in the fields of technical harmonisation, fiscal policy and social affairs all impair the ability of the European industry to compete. A single European currency is an important goal towards which both the Commission and the Member States should be directing their efforts. As Mr Planchon said, "The Commission and national governments must ensure that balanced competitive conditions - a level playing field - prevail in the European Union." Extra costs due to cross-frontier differences hit SMEs, such as the majority of companies in the automotive components sector, the hardest. For this reason Mr Planchon feels it is extremely important to aim the "volet interne" at covering the costs of shedding the differing national structures which are hindering the completion of the single European market.

This first Workshop of the European Parliament / European Commission Forum on the European Automobile Industry provided a platform for all concerned to set out the shape of the restructuring challenge as they see it.

FORUM ON THE EUROPEAN AUTOMOBILE INDUSTRY

BRUSSELS - PALAIS DES CONGRÈS - 1 MARCH 1994

WORKSHOP 2

EUROPEAN PUBLIC POLICY FOR THE CAR INDUSTRY - DEMANDS AND RESPONSES -

Moderator:	Mr A. Richemond	Consultant Economist on Automotive Issues
The Requirements of EU Automotive Producers	Mr L. Schweitzer	Président Directeur général of Renault
The Requirements of EU Component Suppliers	Dr H. Manger	Member of the Board of Robert Bosch GmbH
The Requirements of Labour in the EU	Dr S. Camusso	Secretary for the Car Industry of the Italian FIOM-CGIL Trade Union
European Union Policy	Mr R. Perissich	Director General for Industry, European Commission
Panel:	Mr P. Beazley	Member of the European Parliament
	Mr J. Murray	BEUC, the European Consumer Organisation
	Dr B. Dankbaar	MERIT Economic Research Institute
	Ms E. Kuda	IG-Metall

41

📖 *Mr Richemond:*

Please take your seats as quickly as possible, Ladies and Gentlemen - we are already running late.

Let us begin. I would first of all like to thank Mr Perissich, who has kindly handed over the moderator's seat to me. He has taken his place on the Panel, and has left me the microphone, so that I can moderate this Workshop, and can ensure that the difficulties over the timing of the speeches can be overcome, so that each speaker will have the chance to make a statement.

You may still be frustrated, as indeed I am. I don't know if Carole Tongue is more frustrated than I am, but I think she wanted us to engage in a dialogue here. We heard earlier a series of monologues - very interesting ones - but I think we have some progress to make in achieving a dialogue to try to advance in the definition of what a European policy for the automobile industry could be.

We have seen that the restructuring in the European automobile industry which is going on at the moment has put it back into the black. We must help the manufacturers in their efforts to further the restructuring, and we note that this battle is being won on several fronts. National governments, as well as the institutions of the European Union, are working to define policies to help in this process. They must be helped to define such policies.

Elected representatives are also speaking here today, because they want to protect jobs associated with the automotive industry in their constituencies. The motor vehicle manufacturers, as well as their suppliers, in this, the largest and also the most open of the markets in the world, thereby have a margin for manoeuvre in the sphere of joint ventures, collaboration, etc., without threatening the level of consumer choice. Finally, the Unions, who haven't hesitated to start on the important process of Social Dialogue to face up to the changes taking place in the restructuring European automobile industry.

We have brought all these actors together today, and we want to show them the benefits of such a dialogue. We have Mr L. Schweitzer, Président Directeur général of Renault, who will represent the automobile manufacturers in this Workshop, Dr H. Manger, Member of the Board of Robert Bosch, to represent the component manufacturers, Dr S. Camusso, Secretary for the Automobile Industry of the Italian FIOM Trade Union, and finally the European Commission, represented by Mr R. Perissich, Director General for Industry.

You know the rules of the game - ten minutes each, and I hope you will try to keep to these times, so that we can go on to have a debate on these issues.

So I shall hand over immediately to Mr Schweitzer, President of Renault.

📖 *Mr Schweitzer:*

Ladies and Gentlemen,

First of all, permit me to congratulate the European Parliament and, more particularly, Mrs Carole Tongue and the European Commission, for having organized this Forum on the European Automobile Industry.

This Forum provides a unique opportunity for bringing home to the main players in the automobile industry (including not only, of course, the manufacturers, but also the suppliers, distributors, trade unions and public authorities, be they national or European) that they each have a crucial role to play in assuring the future of this industry.

If only one of these players were to be found wanting, this would be enough to render the future uncertain.

As far as my contribution is concerned, I shall be taking as my theme **"The needs of the manufacturers in the formulation of a European policy for the automobile industry"**.

The **challenge** facing the European automobile industry is **twofold**:

-   to ensure constant progress *vis-à-vis* our **competitive position** in a very difficult environment characterized by the steepest slump in the European market since the Second World War (16% in 1993, followed by the current year, 1994, which hardly appears to be any better) and by international competition of an increasingly cut-throat nature;

-   to satisfy the demands of our customers who crave the **mobility**, and comfort which the modern car **alone** can provide, while at the same time continuing to reduce still further the negative aspects of the car in the area of pollution, congestion, noise and safety.

These two challenges directly concern not only the manufacturers (naturally enough) but also all of our suppliers. For my part, I do not intend to enlarge the scope of my paper to cover changes in the relationship between manufacturers and their subcontractors, since Mr Planchon has already spoken at length on this subject, and the next speaker, Dr Manger, will also be taking up this theme.

I. The challenge of competitiveness

Let us therefore return to the challenge of competitiveness.

Quite clearly, **the primary responsibility for ensuring the competitiveness of their undertakings** rests with **the manufacturers**. It is up to them to ensure technological development and innovation in the field of products, process control, quality of production, efficiency of distribution and customer satisfaction - all at the lowest possible cost.

In facing this challenge, the European automobile industry holds a number of trump cards but also displays a number of weaknesses.

1. The market

The first factor affecting competitiveness is **the market**.

- First of all, on the subject of markets, **the European Union**, with more than 12 million vehicles sold annually, **is the largest market in the world**, outstripping the United States (11 million) and Japan (5 million), and the possibilities for growth, notably in southern Europe, remain considerable. This predominance is also true in terms of production (Europe: 35%, Japan: 25%, US: 25%, rest of the world: 15%).

Lastly, the European Union's balance of trade in the automobile sector has regularly been favourable over the last 10 years (of the order of 20,000 million ecus), whereas the European Union's overall balance has been in deficit (of the order of 30,000 million ecus).

But (and, unfortunately, there are a number of "buts"):

1.1 **Firstly, the Single Market has not been completed**. It is essential, if European industry is to take full advantage of the Single Market, that steps be taken to speed up **tax harmonization and monetary convergence.** In the automobile sector, taxes vary from 15% to 215% in Europe, and differences in the basis of assessment, coupled with critical threshold effects, aggravate the distortions in competition which they create. **In particular, the monetary fluctuations of the past two years** within the Union **have rendered the notion of a single market devoid of any economic sense whatsoever**.

For Renault, the successive devaluations in Italy, Spain and the United Kingdom have had a negative impact of about FF 3,000 million on the 1993 figures and are playing havoc with the distribution networks.

1.2 **Secondly, the European Union's common external policy must be strengthened.**

- There is no justification for allowing South Korea to benefit from the Generalized System of Preferences to the extent that it is able to export 100,000 vehicles to Europe, whereas Korea's imports from Europe are limited to a few hundred a year.

- **The Agreement between the Community and Japan must be applied intelligently but firmly.** The principle of sharing with regard to upturns and downturns in growth **must** be respected and the trade deficit with Japan in the automobile sector progressively reabsorbed. This deficit, alone, is equivalent to more than double the amount of automobile exports to Japan and has been growing continuously over the last few years (+ 25% in 1992).

1.3 **Thirdly, our industry must face up to ever-diminishing and increasingly pronounced economic cycles**. Flexibility and speed of reaction are crucial factors in tackling these situations, and Renault's current strategy is directed less at improving its forecasting tools (which are bound to remain imperfect) and more at creating an organization capable of absorbing variations in the market, such as those which we have experienced in 1993.

For the rest, these cycles prevent us from making optimum use of our industrial capacity.

2. **Products, product quality and technological control**

The second factor determining the competitiveness of our industry concerns the product, its quality and the area of technological control.

Europe has no reason whatsoever to feel ashamed, either of the technological content of its products or of their quality. It is to Europe that credit must be given for the major advances of recent years (injection, ABS, power-assisted steering, automatic gearbox, catalytic converter, etc.). **Europe's technological capability in the automobile sector** is second to none. In 1991, research and development expenditure in Europe amounted to 11,000 million ecus, as against 9,000 million in Japan and 8,000 million in the United States. Furthermore, Europe's automobile knowhow, which is the fruit of multiple technologies, is without equal.

But

-      in the field of research and development going beyond basic research, **European cooperation in global terms is lagging behind** the United States and Japan.

The time is past when the politicians could tell the industry that it must cooperate more and when the industry could tell the politicians that they must establish research-support mechanisms in order to compete with what is going on in the United States and Japan.

The European automobile industry and the public authorities have demonstrated, notably through the Eureka and Drive programmes, their ability to cooperate closely. However, they must now press ahead so as to ensure that the results of this research are transposed more rapidly into an industrialized context.

The manufacturers have presented the Commission with a vast programme of cooperation in the field of research and development, and specific projects are in the pipeline.

For its part, the Commission has developed a more progressive perception of its role in supporting the automobile industry in this area, but **it is still too reserved in its approach to precompetitive and non-sectoral research and with regard to the allocation of funds**, inasmuch as, out of the 13,000 million ecus under the Fourth European Framework Programme, only 1,800 million are to be earmarked for the industrial technologies.

In order to make progress and to avoid being outpaced by Japan and the United States in this area, a pragmatic approach is called for:

- **the Commission and Japan should carry out a more efficient competitive analysis** of what is "really" going on in the United States and Japan between the industry and the public authorities and draw the necessary conclusions;

- **the European automobile industry must speed up** the way in which it defines specific cooperation projects in the various areas that have been identified, and the Commission must be in a position to respond in a swift and meaningful way.

We have talked about the market and the product but, in the area of competitiveness, it is also necessary to look at costs.

3. Economic competitiveness

This is, indeed, a vast area but, for the purpose of our present concerns, it is important that the Commission and Parliament should be in no doubt that **this industry is pursuing** with determination the task of **restructuring itself**, so as to be in a position to face up to international competition at the end of the decade. At the same time, however, it is also important that both the Commission and Parliament should see it as their responsibility to provide the industry with a **political, economic, social and monetary environment which is, itself, competitive.**

It has often been said that the European automobile industry as a whole, i.e., manufacturers and subcontractors, is lagging significantly behind its Japanese and American counterparts. This may well be true, but we should nevertheless avoid making overgeneralizations. Competitiveness among manufacturers operating in the same sector of the triangle is not identical, and positions vary over time, sometimes dramatically so, owing to currency parity changes.

A manufacturer's economic **competitiveness depends on the soundness of his organization** (from the organizational unit on the shop floor to the executive board, and including the organizational unit forming the basis of his distribution network), **on the efficiency of his purchasing policy, on profitability** (in the true sense of the term), **on his investments** and, **lastly, on the efficiency of his labour force**, i.e., on its quality and cost.

Over the last 10 years enormous efforts have been made in these areas by all the manufacturers and subcontractors and by both sides of industry. Personally, I take the view that few non-specialized European manufacturers would have been able 10 years ago to cope with the decline in the market experienced in 1993. While the financial results will hardly be brilliant, they will not be such as to jeopardize the survival of the undertakings.

As an example of the progress made in France, we should recall that in 1980 11 vehicles were produced per employee, whereas, in 1992 the figure had risen to 19.

3.1 Cost and quality of the labour force

In this area of competitiveness, the cost and quality of the labour force are crucial factors, and I would like to dwell on this aspect for a moment, not least because my words today are addressed principally to the Commission and the European Parliament.

- **On the question of labour force costs**, and contrary to certain received ideas, **these costs are not at all unfavourable in global terms** in the context of our European industry: $20 per hour, including social security charges, on average for the countries of the Monetary Union, as against $24 in Japan and $21 in the United States. However, two points need to be made:

    (i) first of all, this average figure covers a wide variety of situations: $28 in Germany, $21 in Belgium, $16 in France, Italy and Spain and $14 in the UK, at the rates of exchange in force at the end of 1993;

    (ii) secondly, **statutory labour charges have grown in the Community by 40% in real terms since 1970**, i.e., twice as fast as in the United States. These statutory charges account for 40% of total labour charges in the Community, whereas in Japan and the United States they represent only 20%. Equally, major discrepancies have been noted within Europe, with the United Kingdom being particularly well placed. This explains, in part, the choice of that country for the establishment of relocated plants.

    Here, too, a harmonization effort by the public authorities is necessary. if Europe is to become a reality.

- **As regards the quality of the labour force**, the industry has had the opportunity to set out, on several occasions, the efforts which it is conducting in the field of training and which are currently in the region of 5% of the total wage and salary bill.

    It is up to us to continue to introduce major changes in our manufacturing systems, in that we have an ageing **unskilled** labour force with a low level of basic training, coupled with the fact that, for a number of years now, the manufacturers have been compelled to limit recruitment of manufacturing personnel.

    In Renault's case, fewer than 15% of workers in 1993 were under the age of 35, and two-thirds of the workforce were over 40. This is a very different situation when compared to the relocated plants, where the average age is found to be in the region of 30.

    In order to achieve this adequate balance between the new manufacturing systems and the qualifications of the personnel, Renault has developed a specific training programme in excess of 1,000 million francs for the coming five years.

- Taking these structures into account, it is essential that the aid in question - whether national or European - should not be unduly biased in favour of new plants at the expense of existing ones. This has not always been the case in the past.

Notwithstanding the undertakings entered into under the "internal section" [volet interne] of the Europe-Japan Agreement, **the resources made available at Community level, both with regard to matters of training and in the area of restructuring, are still either too modest and intricate**, in particular the various specific training programmes (Comett, Force, etc.), **or still lack precision** in terms of their operation, both with regard to the new Structural Fund Objective No 4 on the adaption of workers to industrial change and the Community initiative programmes.

Before concluding this first part of my talk, I should like to stress that everything I have just been talking about (completion of the Single Market at the fiscal and monetary level, pursuit of a more stringent external commercial policy, achievement of greater efficiency as regards research and development programmes) - none of this would have any point if, at the same time, **the European bodies were taking harmful decisions posing dangers to this industry with regard to the protection of industrial property and directly affecting designs and models as well as the system of distribution**. The exclusive and selective system of distribution has shown that it fully satisfies the specific requirements of the automobile sector in line with the price-monitoring mechanisms set up by the Commission. It has also been shown that price differentials in Europe are attributable, primarily, to monetary fluctuations, and not to the system of distribution.

- **The second challenge** which our industry must face concerns the role of the motor vehicle in our daily lives and, here, too, the decisions that are taken in the political arena have a major impact on the automobile industry.

II. The challenge of the social acceptability of the motor vehicle

Three simultaneous constraints are imposed not only on cars but also on lorries (inasmuch as the phenomenon is identical as far as the carriage of goods is concerned):

- **the product must perform its intended function by promoting the mobility** of people under conditions providing for constant enhancements to freedom, availability and safety, given that traffic congestion is continuously on the increase;

- the product must meet the **needs of society as regards the environment and the quality of life**;

- lastly, cars are sold to customers whose resources are finite and for whom price is a crucial factor determining their decision to purchase.

Vast and complex though these subjects are, the public authorities should not lose sight of the third constraint, in so far as any legislative measure of an environmental or fiscal nature which has the effect of increasing the cost of vehicles will have repercussions on the level of demand. However, a reduction in the vehicle replacement rate would not only have serious repercussions for the manufacturers, it would also fly in the face of the environmental and safety concerns which we wish to uphold.

I should merely like to restate two points: the first is an irreversible commitment on the part of the automobile industry to reduce nuisances caused by motor vehicles, and the second is that it is essential that the industry should benefit from **stable and consistent legislation providing sufficiently extended lead times** to allow for the preparation of the appropriate technical solutions.

Let us take two examples: one where considerable progress has been made, i.e., motor vehicle emissions, and another where the essential work has still be done, i.e., transport policy.

1. **On the question of emissions, the industry has demonstrated its commitment to large-scale reductions in emissions**. Vehicles currently being sold in Europe emit 90% less carbon monoxide (CO) and 85% less in unburned hydrocarbons (HC) and nitrogen oxides (NO_x) than vehicles sold in 1970, the year when the first European Directive on emissions came into force. As a result, and taking into account stock replacement forecasts, the European car population will emit 70% less CO and 75% less in HC and NO_x in the year 2010 than at present.

   Lastly, the Commission has proposed the launch, in 1996, of a new stage in the tightening-up process.

   These results are self-explanatory, and it is now time for the Commission and the European Parliament, together with the manufacturers, to draw up a joint definition of a **new approach and the progress still needed**, notably in controlling vehicles in circulation, in providing better driver education facilities and in making available the necessary tools for controlling and improving air quality. The programme of research on fuel improvement, initiated by the automobile and petroleum industries (with Commission involvement) and linked to the various motor vehicle technologies, is an essential step in the right direction. It would be irrational and misleading if new proposals on the reduction of standards were to be decided without waiting for the results of this programme.

2. **On the question of a transport policy and improvements in the traffic situation**, there are two approaches: **one negative, and the other positive**.

   The negative approach is based on the premise that there are too many cars and lorries on the roads and **that steps must be taken to reduce their numbers**, either by limiting their use or by making them more expensive. Quite clearly, the European manufacturers realize that certain town and city centres can and must be closed to traffic and that every effort must be made to promote the effective development of intermodal transport. At the same time, however, they would like to see the introduction of **a transport policy that is more favourable on all fronts: the battle must be waged not against mobility** (mobility is, after all, an essential ingredient of freedom) **but against the negative effects of mobility**. To this end, **better use must be made of the existing infrastructures** and, **where they are inadequate, they must be developed further**. Naturally, there will be a price to pay, but it must be borne in mind that vehicle and fuel sales represent **more than**

ECU 200,000 million in tax receipts per year in Europe, i.e., more than corporation tax. What proportion of this amount has been earmarked for improving the mobility of persons and goods?

As far as the better use of infrastructures is concerned, the manufacturers, the equipment suppliers, the national authorities through the Eureka programmes and the Commission through the Drive programmes **have spent considerable sums on the development of various computerized telecommunication systems for improved traffic management. These systems are ready to run** but first it is necessary to establish the infrastructures needed for the collection and transmission of the information throughout Europe in a coherent and harmonized manner. Steps must also be taken to convince the consumer that the costs are justified by offering genuine improvements in traffic and safety conditions.

Without a major commitment on the part of the national and European public authorities, the hopes vested in telematic road traffic systems will all be to no avail.

In conclusion, my aim is to convince you - over and above the specific measures quoted in the course of this presentation - of the need for greater cooperation among the various actors in the automobile sector, i.e., manufacturers, subcontractors, distribution networks, trade unions and public authorities. More particularly, speaking directly to our hosts, the Commission and the European Parliament, I should like to say that **nowadays our competitors are no longer just companies but entire coherent national systems**. Everybody is aware of the close links that exist between the MITI and Japanese industry, and President Clinton has been at great pains to forge stronger links between the Federal Administration and the automobile industry. Our task is to join together in tackling this new situation by working with both the Commission and Parliament to promote the gradual development of an identical relationship, thus demonstrating that Europe has indeed become a reality.

Thank you very much.

Mr Richemond:

Thank you Mr Schweitzer. Let us turn immediately to Dr Manger, Member of the board of Robert Bosch, speaking here on behalf of the supply of the automotive suppliers.

Dr Manger:

Thank you Mr Chairman. Good morning Ladies and Gentlemen.

What action is needed to improve market conditions in Europe?

The market outlets for suppliers are the motor vehicle manufacturers. The following therefore applies to those suppliers: everything which promotes the sale of cars also helps the supply industry. It should be pointed out here that the suppliers add roughly half of the value to a car.

The manufacturers and suppliers (OEMs) are interdependent. The OEMs are actually attracted to successful vehicle manufacturers in order that their turnover is sufficient to be able to write off the high development and production costs.

In turn the manufacturers need robust suppliers who are in a position further to develop existing products and develop new products in order to maintain the high technical level of the European vehicle industry.

The use of private cars in conurbations is already nearing saturation point. However, we do not see the solution in a restriction of individual transport or in making car driving more expensive. There is no alternative to the motorcar. However, the future lies in the incorporation of the motorcar into a comprehensive traffic management system. Tests involving intelligent traffic management systems show that the load on the existing road network can be significantly increased by using traffic guidance technology. Fluid traffic also makes more ecological sense than traffic at a standstill. The OEM industry is making significant contributions to the expansion of this technology - which in Germany is called telematics - as happened earlier for example in exhaust gas or safety technology.

Quick widespread introduction at European level would be highly desirable and as part of this attempts should be made to standardise on the technology used.

Under current conditions we see no point in making the emission laws already adopted more stringent. The effect on the environment would be very slight whereas cars would become considerably dearer. Tax incentives for the premature removal from the roads of older vehicles not incorporating the more recent exhaust gas clean-up technology would be better.

What action is needed to allow car manufacturers and suppliers to improve their competitiveness in the Community?

Just like the motor vehicle industry the OEMs are also having to bear high costs in some European countries. Major efforts have in recent years been made in several companies in order to improve productivity.

A great deal of effort is also being made, by means of close co-operation with the vehicle manufacturers, to make existing products simpler and reduce the large number of variants. A good example of international co-operation is the mutual recognition of quality audits at suppliers by the various manufacturers in Germany and France.

We feel that the European motor industry is still as robust as ever it was and can therefore do without subsidies and regulations. However we see a considerable need for action on harmonizing the background conditions within Europe. Taxes, environmental protection and safety requirements, technical specifications, etc. should be made uniform within Europe.

However, European plants are competing not only with each other, but also with plants in the Far East, the USA, and in future, in Eastern Europe too. The background conditions must be improved considerably if European plants are to remain competitive.

Key words:

Work period flexibility, machinery operating times, bureaucratic hurdles. All of this requires that monopolies and mergers decisions must be reached no longer in national or European terms, but rather in global terms.

Labour relations:

What action is needed to facilitate the qualitative and quantitative adjustment of the workforce in the car industry?

Can changes be carried out in a harmonious fashion; what is the role of the public authorities in this respect?

Workforce qualification in Europe continues to be very good. However, more flexibility must be required of these in future. It will more frequently happen that the workforce is subject to structural adaptations for which it initially will have not been trained.

We expect that our workforce will undergo constant training and will also be geographically mobile.

It must be possible and financially acceptable for companies to lay off workers where so needed by short-term economic cycles and by any further increases in productivity needed. Redundancy-protection rules as in, for example, Germany and Spain, make such adjustments more difficult and hamper future investments in countries having such laws.

Our machinery must be utilised intensively where production ties up a great deal of capital, e.g. continuous round the clock operation for seven days per week in the case of semi-finished products. The right conditions must be delivered by politicians and the unions.

External trade:

Is the world market a "level playing field" for European car manufacturers? How much emphasis should be given to opening up other world markets?

With differences in emphasis the European motor manufactures supply not only the European, but also the world market. Many of them also produce outside Europe and some even have their home markets outside Europe in either the USA or Japan. The motor industry became world-wide long ago. The same applies to many European OEMs.

In the past the motor vehicle manufacturers and their suppliers were forced into local manufacture in several countries outside Europe by customs regulations or "local-content" requirements. However, these were uncompetitive in international terms because of the small production runs involved. As far as we are concerned, free trade in goods and services is required to ensure the long-term competitiveness of the motor industry. We welcome the incipient liberalisation of imports in some countries, but this must take place in small bites and not over a longish periods in order to make possible any adaptation processes needed.

The OEMs can therefore only advocate a continuation of the GATT process. It is, however, food for thought that the most recent proposals concerning tariff reductions on imports into the EU involve totally different duty rates for passenger cars, commercial vehicles and original equipment. A duty rate of only 3% will expose the OEMs to much sharper global competition than the passenger car manufactures, at 10% and the commercial vehicle manufacturers at up to 19%.

This will sharpen the world-wide competition between OEMs even more. Many OEMs will in future have to give even more careful consideration to locating outside the EU in their future investment planning. On the other hand the European motor industry can only achieve long-term success if it can fall back on a healthy European component supply industry.

This is all I have to say on the questions put. Despite the problems arising for the moment I am convinced that the European motor industry will defend its leading position. We as OEMs will in the future continue to work on regaining lost ground and opening up fresh territory. As hitherto we are basing ourselves on co-operation on a partnership basis with the motor vehicle manufactures and the dialogue with the policy makers' representatives.

Mr Richemond:

Thank you Dr Manger. And now Dr Camusso, who is the Secretary for the Automobile Industry of the Italian FIOM Trade Union, and she will speak on behalf of the Trade Unions. We have already heard Bill Jordan, President of the European Metalworkers' Federation, earlier this morning, and I think that Dr Camusso is going to be able be able to say a little more about the wishes of the partners on her side in the area of restructuring and the public policy to be introduced in the sphere of the European automobile industry. Dr Camusso.

Dr Camusso:

Thank you very much.

I feel that the Commission's initiative in organising this event is very important. It means that we now have an opportunity to talk about the dialogue in our sector. We feel that it should be possible for the Commission and the Parliament to investigate the components of an industrial policy. A great deal has been said about setting up an internal market in Europe, and a great many people have said that a homogenous tax policy is necessary to have an effective policy in this respect. That is probably the starting point for Union policy: rules which are going to make the tax system consistent in all the

Member States, from the cost of fuel, for example, to the notion of a homogenous policy which can be geared to the renewal of the fleet of vehicles in Europe.

So there are instruments to work on. Mr Bangemann described some of these this morning. In the free market, the Union cannot dictate, but can promote. I think of course that there has to be a Social Dialogue, but between all the partners. Up to now the main role of national governments has been to set market quotas, particularly for Japanese producers. However this approach has not tended to produce fiscal policy decisions that favour ecological innovation in the area of car production.

First and foremost we should set great weight upon the need for a competitive system. If the European industry is to compete with Japan and the United States, then we will probably have to go for forms of co-operation on products and components and not just competition between the European companies. From this point of view, using competitive and innovatory capacity, we would be able to keep down our costs, and facilitate something else which can be done at Union level, setting up systems to enable companies to go for long-term policies in areas such as research.

We need to stop trying to restrict the market, and rather focus on winning back and maintaining the competitivity of the European car industry. This is the only way jobs in Europe can be protected in the long term. To this end we need to develop a policy of precompetitive collaboration and a legislative role for the Union favouring planned research and production.

I think we already have a lot of congestion in Europe. There is a conflict between private and public transport. We have to find products which are going to be ecological, acceptable to society, and which are going to make our cities pleasant to live in once again.

The car industry can, and indeed must, play a major role in renewing economic and social development models in the Union. This was the thinking behind the workers' and Unions' initiative during the Fiat dispute that ended a few days ago. The agreement reached between the Government and Fiat - as a result of our initiative - involves forming consortia of companies to conduct research into ecological vehicles, electronic traffic-control and traffic-safety systems, the recovery of components after scrapping and the recycling of materials. This is the way forward, one favouring collaboration between producers, rules and regulations, defining targets and objectives.

The car industry used to be a major producer and employer. No solution has been found to excess productive capacities in Europe and the world in general, apart from looking for new markets. New working hours need to be introduced, reducing significantly the individual's working week. Flexibility issues should also be tackled from the viewpoint of auto-organization and auto-management of manual and technical work. European policies in this direction need to be agreed.

We cannot talk exclusively of costs, however. It is possible, above all to look at non-wage costs, as Mr Garuzzo said earlier. One must choose to go for quality of work. The quality of work and the quality of product probably go together. The policy of the EU has been quite strong on funding projects and on training, and this should continue.

The organizational models of production, the level of innovation which will still be necessary, already point to the limits of lean production, the need which a better mode of working provides for ongoing training and agreed forms of initiative on work organization.

Mr Richemond:

Thank you Dr Camusso.

Mr Perissich, as Mr Schweitzer has asked, from the perspective of a manufacturer, an employee or a consumer in Europe, do you think that it is a handicap or an advantage to belong to a union of states?

Mr Perissich:

That is a good question, Mr Chairman.

When one speaks of the role of public policy in such a complex operation as the restructuring of the European car industry, one has to bear in mind Mr Schweitzer's question. Most, or many of the actions which can be carried out by public authorities - and that can have a bearing on the restructuring of the European car industry - are in fact the exclusive, or at least primary, responsibility of the Member States. Anything related to labour costs, working conditions, the labour market, lies perhaps not exclusively, but primarily, in national hands. Other key areas that have been identified by previous speakers as having a strong impact, like monetary movements, or fiscal harmonisation, are all areas where the Union solidarity is in progress, but we all know how difficult it is to make it grow. It is therefore not surprising that when we speak from the point of view of the Commission we focus on those areas where we can actually do something ourselves, but we should also be conscious of the fact that we cannot control the whole picture.

Finally, one has to bear in mind that almost everything that can be done by the Community is focused on the medium to long term. The Community is not very good at short term issues. The Member States are better placed to do something in the short term.

Having said that, I should like to concentrate on just two or three points.

1. Horizontal approaches to industrial policy do not mean lack of focus for particular industries.

The first concerns the familiar debate within the Commission and industry on horizontal versus sectoral approaches. What we are experiencing at the moment is a global restructuring of the whole economic system. In this global restructuring there are no special industries. The type of restructuring that we are experiencing concerns the whole European and worldwide manufacturing system, and so such approaches have to be developed in a horizontal way.

The Union's approach is to create a favourable business environment supporting industrial competitivity and industrial restructuring. This has to be done within a horizontal policy framework, without favouring one industry over another.

The United States is alleged to be following a different approach after years eschewing sectoral industrial policy. The "Green Car" or "New Generation Vehicle" research initiative is a sector-specific action in favour of one industry. This has led to demands for a comparable programme in the EU. Let us examine this point.

Firstly, the "Green Car"' programme is not a single research action but many actions under one umbrella. The main innovation is the attempt to exploit the resources of the massive defence research base to the benefit of the auto industry.

In Europe our research efforts are more difficult to co-ordinate. Yet taken together, the industry's target research efforts are very similar, if not identical, to those of US industry. The aim in brief is to research the development of a **"clean, lean-produced, environmentally friendly, quality, value"** car for the year 2000 and beyond.

What is needed in Europe is **"focus"** within horizontal programmes on long-term aims. This focus should be such as to ensure that the maximum benefits are derived from synergies with other industries and technologies, and that integrated research proposals are treated as "homogeneous" wholes and not as ad hoc actions with no thematic focus. Here the Commission has an important role to play in ensuring co-ordination amongst programme managers and coherence of approach.

The industry, through its new research and development arm "EU-CAR", could facilitate these co-ordination efforts by presenting us with a chart showing how each research action fits in with the long-term aim.

With respect to using **structural funds,** the focus is even clearer. In particular the emphasis in Objective 4 and ADAPT and PME, the new Community Initiative Programmes, on actions to promote training for workers affected by changes in production systems and to encourage training links between SMEs and downstream assemblers, is to be highlighted. These priorities correspond to key problems identified in the automotive sector. It is now up to companies and their workforces to take the necessary measures to ensure that national authorities take account of their needs when presenting their proposals for Community Support Frameworks.

2. The need for regulatory stability

The institutions of the Union have heard the call from the industry for regulatory stability. This needs to be translated into consistent policy making practice.

Two examples illustrate this point.

(i) Selective and Exclusive Distribution

The text adopted by the Commission in the Communication recognises the specificity of the automobile industry. The need for a swift decision on how the Regulation will be applied in the future is fully recognised by the Commission on the grounds that it is important to provide planning stability for the industry and the 1.1 million people working in the authorised distribution chains. The need to encourage better partnership relations between all elements of the distribution chain is also recognised as an important element of industrial competitivity, as is the key role that the Regulation plays in the efficient management of the arrangement with Japan on automobiles.

In brief, the text adopted will ensure that the regulations in the distribution sector are stable and not subject to abrupt and disruptive change.

(ii) Car emissions

The Commission is very conscious of the fact that the introduction of new environmentally-clean technologies to reduce car emissions require the industry to be given sufficient lead time to make the necessary investments in order to meet the new standards. We are also aware that we are reaching the limit in terms of what can be achieved in terms of just acting on engine technologies alone. That is why the Commission proposed that in the next stage - "Etape 2000" - a multi-faceted approach should be taken to reducing emissions with a cost-benefit analysis to be made of all potential contributory measures to reducing car emissions including improved engines, improved fuels, better inspection and maintenance of vehicles, improved traffic management, etc. This approach is being underpinned by the Auto-Oil programme, a unique effort by the car and petroleum industries in conjunction with the Commission to see the effects on emissions that can result from improved engine technologies and improved fuels. This is an important research programme - albeit one in its infancy - and it should not be jeopardised by actions by the Institutions.

While the Council and the Commission are on the same lines as regards the next stage for reducing emissions, and have moved significantly in the direction of the approach desired by the Parliament, the same cannot be said about the European Parliament itself, which next week will debate the car emissions Directive in its second reading. Before the Parliament will be a series of amendments which are quite simply unattainable in industrial terms and which would put the Auto-Oil programme at risk. Most importantly the amendments before the Parliament would have the effect of creating a multiplicity of regulatory standards in the market - 1991,1996, 1999 and post 2000, with all the confusion in terms of the internal market that this will entail.

While we in the Commission would like future policy actions in the automotive sector to be judged against what we have said in our Communication on the European Automobile Industry, we believe the European Parliament should base its actions on its own "equivalent" recent report on the car industry, namely the "Tongue" report which was adopted by the Parliament in November 1993.

You cannot facilitate industrial restructuring in an environment of regulatory instability; yet this would be the consequence of adopting the amendments to the car emissions directive now before the Parliament. I would urge therefore that the Parliament in its consideration of this matter follows the logic of Carole Tongue's report.

3. The need to open markets

A major theme in our Communication is the need for the industry to take advantage of new high-growth markets in order to diversify away from its current predominantly regional European focus. To some extent it could be said that in geographical terms the EU industry is better placed than its United States counterpart. Eastern European markets are on our doorstep, and whilst potential there is limited for the time being, the long-term prospects are much better. These are markets with very low motorisation levels. Increased sales opportunities will also occur in Turkey whose market will more than double between now and the end of the century.

Further afield, the prospects in Asia and China are for fast growth of markets. European manufacturers cannot afford not to be present on these markets.

In many of them barriers exist to market penetration and investment. It should be a major priority of the Union to remove these so as to facilitate market access. This goes as well for more developed markets such as Japan and the USA where, as our report highlights, there are still barriers to EU sales.

We receive much useful information from the ACEA and others on the **existence of market barriers** but much less on where the priorities lie. We need to establish jointly a **joint priority list** which should act as a reference point for action. For this we need the industry's support. So we would invite ACEA and CLEPA to tell us what your market opening priorities are.

Thank you very much for your attention, ladies and gentlemen.

Mr Richemond:

Thank you Mr Perissich. I already have several questions sent up from the floor of the Forum which I shall shortly be putting to you.

We shall start this round table debate with Mr Beazley, Member of the European Parliament.

Mr Beazley:

Thank you Mr Chairman.

I want to ask, what are the overall problems which the motor car industry faces today?

European public policy is what we're talking about today, and the industry must base its policy on markets, both European and world, not just ten, but twenty years ahead. Given that a particular car type lasts for some ten years, Europe is at present facing a sea change both in the market and in the technology and production requirement to meet costs and competition. Not just Japan, but South East Asia's very much cheaper labour market.

So, in which direction should the European auto industry move its technology and its manufacturing costs? Currently it's moving upwards in technological terms very fast, and thus in cost terms too, reflected in motor car prices.

European roads even today and certainly in the future will not be able to cope with the volume of cars and trucks which European consumers and business will demand. Should we not be working now on designing new style cars for the world of 2000-2020? Should the motor industry not prepare itself now for competition with the cars conforming to the desires of society in the future?

Thank you.

Mr Richemond:

Thank you. Mr Murray?

Mr Murray:

Thank you. As you know, I represent the independent national consumer organisations from all the Member States of the Union, and also from most of the EFTA countries, and I should like to thank the Parliament and the Commission for inviting me here today. I'm also glad, ladies and gentlemen, that panellists are allowed to sit down, because a lot of what I'm going to say may not be very popular, and I present a smaller target when I'm sitting down!

Certainly I do have to say that looking at the overall list of participants that one might be forgiven for finding it difficult to believe that the purpose of production is consumption.

The challenge facing industry is the challenge of giving consumers cars of the quality and the price that they want to buy. We believe that this can only be achieved by creating competitive conditions in the European market, and we think that there is not enough competition in this area at present. We are certainly a long way from achieving the Single Market where consumers can move freely throughout the territory, buy a car, and bring it home. Some of the reasons we don't have a Single Market, the fiscal and monetary reasons, have already been mentioned, but there are very many other factors which are in our control. We still have too much of the legacy of the old policy of promoting national champions. We still have too much in the way of protectionist policies and protectionist mentalities at national levels within the market.

The market for cars in the Union is segmented, in some cases by the actions of national administrations, in some cases by the continuing existence of an exclusive distribution system, which gives industry at all levels an interest in maintaining the status quo. More recently, another influence towards segmentation was the so-called EC-Japan Consensus, which implies continued restrictions on the movement of cars across borders within the Union.

So the first point I would make is that any policy you are discussing is doomed to failure if it is based on a false sense of self-congratulation on the degree to which a competitive market has been achieved within the European Union. We are a long way from that market yet.

On selective distribution, you may know that we think the present system should be scrapped in order to prevent greater segmentation of the market, and in order to promote greater competition. Mr Bangeman seems to think it should be maintained. At least he said he thought it should be maintained before he'd even heard the case for scrapping it, but he made an even worse argument today, on which I would like to comment briefly. There are many bad arguments for maintaining the present system. The worst is that it is needed in order to maintain the continuing restrictions on movements across frontiers under the terms of the EC-Japan consensus.

My second point, Mr Chairman, is that future policy will also be doomed to failure if it fails to take into account the <u>full</u> costs of protectionism and restrictions to competition. In the late eighties for example, it was calculated that the full cost of the restrictions on Japanese car imports was around ECU 1,800 on each Japanese car sold in the Community. In a more recent study carried out for the UK national consumer council, it was estimated that the total cost to consumers of the current EC-Japan accord will amount to something like ECU 35 billion over the life of the agreement. Much of that will go to American and Japanese producers who benefit from the higher prices on the European market.

My final point is that we must, when looking at restrictions on competition and protectionism, we must look at the full cost. There must not be some vague assumption that these lead to better employment, better regional policy or whatever. There must be a clear and transparent examination of all the costs, and indeed the benefits, if there are any, but certainly of all the costs of restrictions of competition and protectionist policies.

Thank you Chairman.

Mr Richemond:

Thank you very much. I think it would be dangerous in the context of this debate to only look at one aspect of the automobile industry. To look at a single example, I think that the recovery observable in the large American producers, their achieving significant profit levels, is due to their restructuring, their fast turnover of models, but equally it is due to the devaluation of the Dollar against the Yen, which adds 250 dollars to the cost of a Japanese vehicle on the United States market. This has helped too. I would like us to take a global look, and not just look at single aspects.

We now have Dr Ben Dankbaar, of MERIT Economic Research Institute in Maastricht, who can give us a perhaps more academic look at the issues that have been raised so far in this Workshop.

📔 *Dr Dankbaar:*

Thank you. If you are asked to appear on a Panel such as this, then I suppose you have to explain the role of an academic, and I guess that is to bring some order into the affair. The second role is to make research proposals, because that's what I earn my money from!

I think if we try to make some sense of all the problems and the policies we have been presented with today, and there are more to come, it is useful to differentiate between the time horizons which are valid for these issues individually. It would be useful to distinguish between short-term restructuring and policies, the medium-term research and development policies, and I would also like to say something about long-term visions, because as an academic, you're allowed to be a little un-practical!

What can public authorities do to improve the European business environment for the car industry? In view of the considerable difficulties that the car industry has encountered by the contraction of the market in the course of 1992/1993, there is presently a tendency to focus on policy measures supporting the industry in its short-term efforts to restore competitiveness. Such measures can no doubt be useful, but to enhance their impact it would be wise to put them into a longer-term perspective. I would therefore like to start with some remarks on policies for the long and medium-term, before commenting on measures needed in the next few years.

1. The long term: beyond 2010

What we need is a long-term vision of mobility in Europe and the role of automobility therein. Even the most fervent proponents of automobility will nowadays concede that environmental concerns as well as spatial limitations impose definite limits on the further expansion of the use of automobiles in Europe. On the other hand, it is equally clear that the individual ownership and use of cars is going to remain an important feature of European styles of living in the foreseeable future. For the long-term development of cars and the car industry, it is clearly necessary that new ideas are developed concerning the lay-out of cities and larger urban areas; the frequency and modes of transportation needed between homes, shops and work-places; the interfaces between public transportation systems and private automobility; the size and character of the various vehicles needed for various functions. A vision of mobility in the future will have to guide the public authorities in formulating their policies as well as the product strategies of enterprises. The European Commission would provide a great service to the industry if it organised an open debate on future mobility. Such a debate might or might not end with consensus. In the end, several distinct visions may coexist. Debate of itself would help all parties concerned to identify the issues at stake, and to develop answers to each other's questions and arguments. One way to begin a debate is to invite several known experts to write some substantive position papers independently from each other and to organise a round table discussion about the papers.

2. The medium term (5-15 years)

In the medium term, there is widespread agreement about the road that needs to be followed. We need cleaner and better recyclable cars and we need traffic management systems that reduce pollution by fighting congestion. The public authorities can support research and development efforts in these directions and where this seems useful they can support co-operative efforts in this field. Some of the research needed will be highly specific to the automobile industry, but it will also be important to support the development of European capabilities in some of the relevant generic technologies, especially in electronics.

Another important task for public authorities lies in the field of regulation and standardisation. Regulation needs to push for world-class performance and at the same time provide a stable planning environment for the industry. Standardisation is needed, wherever national and enterprise-specific developments tend to prevent a speedy introduction of innovations. This seems to be the case for instance in traffic management systems, where the technology is basically available, but disagreements on standards prevent implementation.

In the medium term, it will also be necessary for the European car manufacturers to put more resources into the development of new export markets. The markets in both Eastern Europe and the developing regions in other parts of the world, for instance, may offer openings for small, robust trucks of a kind for which European manufacturers seem to have accumulated less expertise than their Japanese and North American competitors.

Research and development needs to be done, and lots has been said about it. Research and development, technical standardisation, particularly in the field of traffic management, and technologies in support of clean cars. There may be much more potential than we think in developing technologies for cars destined for newer markets. Very little has been said about the lack of export capabilities of the European enterprises so far. It may be that we will have to develop new cars for developing countries.

Mr Richemond:

Could you be more explicit? You're being too academic. What kind of projects?

Dr Dankbaar:

I think there is a need for cars which on the one hand are advanced in their technologies, using technologically-advanced management systems for their engines, but which on the other hand are easy to repair and to handle in countries which lack the infrastructure we have here in Europe. These cars are currently not being produced by us. We have no tradition in light trucks, like they have in the United States and in Japan. We're missing out, and I think we can do more here than we are right now. I hope this is not too being academic.

3. The short term: towards the year 2000

Until the end of the century the main worry of the industry and a major concern for policy will be restructuring in the face of strong and growing competition. Policy measures to create a larger demand (e.g. by lowering car-specific taxes) can be useful, because it is easier to restructure in a growing market. Environmental considerations, however, point into another direction. It should be recognized that there is little political desire for a quickly growing car park in Europe.

Many jobs have been lost in the industry in the recent past, more will be lost in the coming years and we have to assume that most of them will not come back, even if the market improves. The burden of restructuring could be greatly reduced if an ample supply of new jobs could be created. The structural funds of the Community will have to be used to create jobs outside the auto industry and consequently will not go to the auto industry itself. This is only logical, and is especially important where the auto-industry is characterised by the existence of large complexes in regions that have never found it necessary to diversify into other economic activities.

Does that mean that the car manufacturers will not need direct support in the restructuring process? There is a definite need to invest in costly training efforts and the industry will welcome support for these actions. In this respect, however, the car manufacturers are already better off than the first and second tier suppliers, who have to take on more responsibility for product development, quality and logistics. In that respect, actions in support of restructuring should take a supply chain perspective and cover both the car manufacturers and all their supplier industries.

It is important to note that restructuring may still involve investment in new capacity by some manufacturers. Although it does seem illogical, it would not be wise to stop manufacturers from investing in new capacity and new locations with the argument that capacity is still available at other manufacturers and other locations. The price of such a policy could be very high, because it would prevent further modernisation by the leading manufacturers of the continent. Of course, the opposite would also be illogical. Support for the establishment of additional capacity, let alone by non-European manufacturers, can hardly be considered a good way to spend public monies.

The restructuring of a large industry is a complex social and political process, requiring a lot of creativity from all parties concerned. In that respect it is sometimes disappointing to see that European management displays very little creativity in their efforts to emulate the successes of their competitors. There is a strong tendency to follow various fashionable concepts launched in the North American business press. Even the lessons from the Japanese industry are often acquired by reading the works of American authors, who necessarily see the Japanese experience through American glasses. The European Commission would probably contribute a great deal to a successful restructuring of the industry if it would encourage the elaboration, systematic description of European approaches in the modernisation and restructuring of industrial organisations. European industries have developed their own styles, organizational models and management traditions, which often are more elaborate and subtle than many of the buzzwords coming to us from the United States. Special attention also needs to be paid to the industrial relations context in Europe, which is not only highly diverse, but also quite different from the context in other parts of the world. Neglect of the specificities of the industrial relations dimension in Europe could be fatal to the success of restructuring efforts. The European Commission can therefore also support the restructuring process by promoting a dialogue between the social partners in the various Member States and at the European level.

On the problems associated with short-term restructuring, it is obvious that we are finally witnessing efforts by the European industry to come to terms with the fact that productivity standards in the industry worldwide have changed. It has taken a long time. It is obvious that many jobs are going to be lost, and this means that the restructuring policies will have to be concerned with creating new jobs, and these are not going to be in the auto industry. In that sense I think it is not going to be un-understandable that the funds that Mr Bangemann referred to today are not all going to the car industry, which some of you are going to be disappointed to hear. That's what he wanted you to think, of course, but in fact most of the restructuring funds will, I hope, be used for the creation of other jobs, and I think it is only right and practical that much of this funding will be administered at a regional or national level, because the problems will be different in different locations. We need policies that can deal with the variety of problems that will arise from the dismissal of tens of thousands of workers in different countries and in different firms. Of course, some jobs will remain in the industry, and some new ones will be created, particularly at the supplier end. I think that much of the restructuring monies that will go into the car industry will need to go into the supplier firms, where more training is needed, and where more technological expertise has to be built up, in order for them to be able to meet the requirements of the assemblers, and also to give them an improved ability to supply other industries.

Another observation I would like to share is in connection with other restructuring problems. It is about overcapacity. Looking for example at the steel industry, where the restructuring policy was used to prevent the restructured firms from investing in new capacity. The result was sufficient capacity, but in the wrong areas. The upshot was that a couple of years later that the best practice firms were no longer best practice firms because they had been prevented from investing in new capacity. Overcapacity may be a problem, but let's not stop the best firms from investing in enlarged capacity.

Finally, on the long term, and that was only a joke to say that this is un-practical. We need visions that go further than traffic management systems. These will help make better use of the infrastructure, but the infrastructure will always remain limited. We need to look much more broadly at mobility. How can we make the most of it? How can we interact with the means of transportation? How can we improve the interface between our transport systems? I think there is scope for a wider debate and some research on the future of mobility in the 21st century, and I can definitely see a role for the Commission there.

Thank you.

Mr Richemond:

I would like to hand over directly to Mrs Eva Kuda, of IG-Metall.

☐ Ms Kuda:

Thank you very much.

Above of all I would like to look at how the elements of a European strategy for training and retraining can be shaped for those employed in the European automobile industry. Everyone has underlined the central role played by skills and qualifications in terms of future competitiveness. Some have spoken of the new requirements of flexibility, creativity, and the ability to work in teams, and to think differently. All of these elements point to the need to upgrade standards in the industry.

We have heard Mr Bangeman speak of improvements in skills being the foremost requirement for the protection of our jobs. The solution to crises in the European automobile industry and in other industries depends on this, but I wonder to what extent the reality of training and further training in the European automobile industry has been implemented. Two or three years ago, IG-Metall collaborated in the organisation of a survey on the whole of the European automobile industry, and the results showed that work in the automobile industry is still work for unskilled persons. There is very little further training.

Germany is taken as a model as regards training, and yet in the automobile industry we have only 3 % retraining at present, and this is declining because of the excessive cost of training and further training. Furthermore, and we shouldn't discourage this, we have a number of models and highly developed forms of skills, training for which is only available to specific groups in the workforce. Innovative approaches will have to be taken in the upgrading of skills. The problem which one has to grasp is that we need a comprehensive upgrading of skills. At the moment measures in this respect are only focused on small portions of the workforce. We cannot look at training and further training as a factor in isolation, otherwise the crisis in the European automobile industry would only be one of training and skills. We think that a further problem has to be grasped, in connection with the need to improve skills. There is the question of the extent to which skilled employees are at all able in the present work structures to apply their skills. This is why some of the employees are complaining about the fact that the know-how they have acquired cannot be applied, leading to the extensive deficiencies in the work structures of our industry.

What conclusions can we draw from this? What demands can we put on a European strategy as regards training and further training in the European auto industry?

We think it is crucial to reinforce innovative competitiveness. The skills of all employees have to be improved, and training has to be made available not just to a few groups, but to all. This a lead to a common effort to find solutions.

Another area is to develop skills which are forward-looking, for people who are going to lose their jobs in the automobile industry. The question of skills has to be focused on these two aspects of the automobile industry.

Thank you.

Mr Richemond:

Thank you, Ms Kuda. The first question which I have received is from Mr Beger, Executive Secretary of the ACEA.

Mr Beger:

We are grateful to Mr Murray for pointing out that the Europe-Japan agreement is not a good reason for justifying selective distribution. We have enough good reasons for justifying selective distribution, however.

Now, we were discussing that partnership is the key to European competitiveness. If selective distribution were destroyed, there would no longer be a basis for any partnership, because there is no co-operation between manufacturers and supermarkets. Is Mr Murray really asking for handicaps to be added to the difficult restructuring situation that the European automobile industry is in?

Mr Murray:

I thought I made my views on this very clear. The selective distribution system is a restriction on competition. Everybody here seems to be in favour of competition, and pretends that there is competition in this area, that we have a competitive market, and so on, and yet, with a few exceptions like me, all of us here want these restrictions on competition. There can be partnerships between all kinds of people, but they turn very quickly into cartels if they are not carefully monitored. The restrictions to competition under the Exemption Regulation should be removed.

Mr Richemond:

We have another question addressed more to Mr Perissich. European industry is eligible for aid from the European Structural Funds, and the impression given was that all the funds which have been made available through recent initiatives would be available for the European automobile industry. Could you please explain how this is supposed to work, and what the relationships are which should be forged between national governments, the Commission, and the sector as a whole.

Mr Perissich:

If anybody gave the impression that all the money would be available for the automobile industry, then he made a slight mistake. Indeed, as there is no sectoral priority, and I explained why there isn't earlier, funds are available for everybody. Another good reason why they should be available for everybody was also given a few moments ago by Dr Dankbaar: most of the restructuring will have to open the way to re-employment in other sectors. Having said that, the various initiatives that exist to aid restructuring and reconversion at Community level embodied in the Structural Funds - and there are a whole range of these funds - all have criteria, and a varying degree of regional specificity. At the end of the day, they imply the implementation of programmes by industry itself, in co-operation with the Member States. The Community, or the Commission, can introduce, and indeed does introduce in the regulations various criteria for eligibility, but it is up to the Member States to take them up. The latest proposal that we made last week, particularly on training and retraining and on Objective 4 are probably the most innovative ever put forward by the Commission, but if at the end of the day, industry and the Member States do not take up these innovative elements, nothing much will happen.

Mr Richemond:

I have a question on the Communication from the Commission on the European Automobile Industry. The Commission, working from a very easy premise, is asking European manufacturers to try to conquer markets abroad. I would like to draw Mr Murray's attention to the fact that the European market is the most open market in the world, and also has the highest level of competition. We have no lessons to learn on competition from anyone else.

I would like to ask Mr Perissich, does this give us any room to manoeuvre in setting up a public policy? I refer here to what said earlier - and can we be more specific about joint projects which can be developed as regards technology, but also perhaps outside markets. In moving towards export markets, don't you think that we also need a strong territorial base? How can we be sure of this, when we have seen that it has taken the European manufacturers a number of years to re-conquer this one?

📖 *Mr Perissich:*

If we start with the assumption that competition is global, then we have to acknowledge that the United States car industry is a global industry, that the Japanese car industry is increasingly a global industry, and that European industry is not. This is a point of weakness. One of the messages we tried to send in our Communication is that we must be prepared to be much more active in terms of exports and investment in new growth markets, which are not going to come from Europe, nor from the United States, nor from Japan. It is going to come from other markets in many of which our presence is weak. One of our best assets is that some of these future growth markets, although we are still not reaping the benefits, will be in Eastern Europe. This is on our back door, and many of us have been investing very actively there, but we have still to see any of the real benefits from these markets.

Now, if we are to expand on these potentially high growth markets, including the United States and Japan, is what we at the Commission can do about it really a priority objective? When one looks at the import regulations of a country like Korea, one cannot help being shocked. There is probably a lot that governments at both national and Community level can and should do to open up these markets - Korea, India, Brazil, and similar markets. Personally, I believe that this should be a priority for Community institutions. Equally, we all know that there are obstacles to Community exports both to Japan and to the United States. Concerning the United States, we have already taken action in the GATT against some of the restrictions in the United States. As regards Japan, we all know that it is much more difficult to pin the Japanese down on specific obstacles, though certainly we should keep up the pressure. Someone said earlier this morning that we should copy the current American approach to the Japanese car and car components market. I don't think this is a good idea. The Commission has repeatedly expressed both scepticism about the effectiveness of such an approach, and also considerable fear that if anything happens it would be at our own expense rather than that of Japan.

Lastly, we should give considerable attention to co-operative programmes, possibly with the United States or the Japanese car industries, on component suppliers. Examples exist. It may help enormously to strengthen the European component supplier base. We have launched successful programmes with the Japanese in Europe in other sectors, such as in consumer electronics. We tend to believe that this area could be promising, both to strengthen the competitive base on our own market, and to increase export potential for European industry in third markets.

You said that if we want to increase our export potential we must be strong on our own market. I would like to remind you even at the end of the transitional period when the European market will be totally open to Japanese imports, European export producers will control a much larger share of the European market than the "Big Three" American producers are able to control at present.

Thank you.

📖 ***Mr Murray:***

You seem to hold a theory of industrial policy which, to put it mildly, is open to question. There are other analyses which are possible. Phillips, which proceeded according to the sorts of policy you seem to be advocating, is now in some difficulty. I think what is needed, to be a world leader, is to have a base in a competitive market, and, because of national segmentation, the European market is not competitive. Also this is due to partnerships between dealers and manufacturers. This keeps dealers weak, and does not allow for strong and independent dealers, who would be a good source of strong independent competition in the European market. We don't have a single market, we have a segmented market, and therefore we don't have conditions in Europe from which European manufacturers can take on the world.

Mr Richemond:

We have heard the manufacturers speak earlier of the costs of "Non-Europe", and I'm thinking here of the tax differences and fluctuations and discrepancies in the rates of exchange.

📖 ***Mr Beazley:***

I would like to address this subject if I may, Mr Chairman, and I would like to say that I was the person who brought this motor industry business into the discussions in the Economic and Monetary Affairs Committee, and I did it as a person who has spent his life in international industry. Becoming a politician, I was concerned about what the wealth creation base was, and I looked at a whole lot of industries, and I came to the motor industry, and I saw it as one which could be saved, but otherwise would not be saved if we went along the way we were going fifteen years ago. I believe that it did have the possibility of generating wealth, of producing work, and actually of being one of our very important industries. I was a most unpopular person in the European Parliament for having proposed it, I might say, but things have moved correctly in this direction, but we still have a very protected market.

Renault was state owned. It is now about 20 % independent, I believe, perhaps even more, it is forward looking. One of the main hold-ups in the development of the motor industry has been this protection of Europe, and the division of Europe. We have to go forward.

I was asked some fifteen years ago if it was worth maintaining a motor industry. There were certain industries that we just had to give up because we were never going to compete with the Japanese or with anyone else. Now we have a most interesting movement, in which we are seeing German companies, which were always producing single style, high quality cars, have now changed their policy and they're moving into another market, but surely we must have openness, we must have competition, and as I've tried to say, but no-one has raised the point, we must look to the future, and because models last for some ten or twelve years, it's now that we ought to be preparing for employment, for the right sort of car for the year 2020.

Mr Richemond:

Thank you very much Mr Beazley, thank you everyone for your attention.

We are finishing some five minutes late and I apologise for this. Please give the participants in this Workshop a round of applause, and thanks also please to Carole Tongue, upon whose initiative this event was organised.

WORKSHOP 2

SUMMARY REPORT

MR A. RICHEMOND
CONSULTANT ECONOMIST

The issues raised in the round table section of this workshop has been that of the interest in having a European common policy for the automobile sector. The actors in this industry, the manufacturers, the unions, the suppliers and the consumers were represented so that their views on the need for, and the shape of, a policy for the car industry could be expressed.

One point was shared by the car manufacturers and the component suppliers. Industry in the wide sense is fully responsible for the restructuring already achieved to improve their level of competitiveness in the global marketplace.

The car manufacturers, like the component suppliers, have been asking themselves what the cost of "non"-Europe would be. The fluctuations in the exchange rates in the European Union, and the differences in indirect taxation policies cause significant imbalances between European partners ...

The issue raised by the industry is that of being able to compete on a level playing field. The efforts of each individual manufacturer are being made to reduce the part the performance of their means of production plays in their overall competitiveness. The public authorities should also throw their weight behind evening the conditions for competition at European level.

Today, the industry is asking itself whether **belonging to a union of states is a handicap or an advantage** as regards giving the industry an economic and regulatory environment in which it can put to use the efforts it has made since the end of the eighties.

The Social Partners insist on the need to find new forms of sharing the existing work. In fact, the unions want to keep the level of employment in the industry and at the same time contribute to raising the level of competitiveness. For this they are also asking for more training. Their concern is that "Lean Production" might lead to a lowering of professional qualifications. According to them, the European public authorities have a role to play in promoting a new automobile industry, more in harmony with the environment.

The Commission, represented by the Director General for Industry, recalled its commitment to putting into action "horizontal" accompanying measures, but no "sectorial" measures at all. The Commission commitment is threefold:

- the Commission must achieve the completion of the internal market;

- the Commission must aid structural transformation;

- the Commission must help those enterprises which are performing the best.

At the same time, the Commission appeared to reject the idea of federating European research and development efforts in projects close to the marketplace, such as exist in the United States of America and in Japan. These joint efforts could be extended to cover infrastructures as well (telematic traffic management, etc.). Only 10 % of the Union's research programmes concern the automobile sector ...

It is essential that the European public authorities should accompany the restructuring efforts that the European manufacturers have been making. The participants in the debate noted the shortcomings of the internal measures ("volet interne") in Union policy. They noted with regret the additional obstacles put in their way just at the moment they were making the greatest of efforts, such as over the selective distribution issue. They shared the diagnosis of Martin Bangemann on the imperative to conquer new markets, and they wanted also to be able to count on a more solid territorial base from which to export and transplant abroad. The internal market is the most open to international competition. The European public authorities therefore have **room to manoeuvre which they are not using**. The wide opening of the market is a guarantee against all attempts to distort competition in favour of the European automobile industry too significantly.

FORUM ON THE EUROPEAN AUTOMOBILE INDUSTRY

BRUSSELS - PALAIS DES CONGRÈS - 1 MARCH 1994

WORKSHOP 3

THE CAR INDUSTRY AND THE REGIONS
- THE MANAGEMENT OF CHANGE -

Moderator:	Mr K.H. Mihr	Member of the European Parliament
The Effects of Restructuring on the Regions	Professor K. Morgan	Department of City and Regional Planning, University of Wales, Cardiff
EU Policy for Adaptation	Mr M.-E. Dufeil	Assistant to the Director General for Regional Policy, European Commission
The Experience of Industry	Dr B. Adelt	Member of the Board of Volkswagen AG
Management of Change at a Regional Level	Sr. Don Pascual Maragall	Mayor of Barcelona
Panel:	Dr C. Camerana	Deputy Chairman of the Board of Magneti Marelli
	Dr K. Benz-Overhage	Member of the Board of IG-Metall
	Ms B. Ernst de la Graete	Member of the European Parliament
	Mr C. Firth	MILAN regional authority network

📖 *Mr Mihr:*

Good afternoon, ladies and gentlemen. Let us begin the third Workshop in this Forum on the European Automobile Industry, which is entitled "The Car Industry and the Regions - The Management of Change".

Before we begin, though, let me quote a headline from a newspaper from this morning on the traditional manufacturers in Europe, which says something which could be applied to most automotive production locations. "Region Breathes Sigh of Relief." This week it has been decided that the small model of a particular series is going to be produced in the local area concerned: This has had some repercussions on the monostructural approach, although the town council has announced that the monostructure has recently improved. It is therefore absolutely necessary to consider the need for an anticipatory industrial policy.

To speak on this topic I should like to welcome Professor Morgan of Cardiff University, an expert on industrial innovation and regional development.

📖 *Professor Morgan:*

In the spirit of lean production I shall endeavour to give a lean presentation.

1. Introduction

Will the auto regions of today suffer the same fate as the coal and steel regions of yesterday? Thinking the unthinkable, could the Greater Stuttgart area, one of the key centres of the auto industry in Europe, become the Ruhrgebiet of the 21st century? Such questions are being asked because a new regional division of labour may be emerging in the European auto industry.

If the precise spatial configuration is unclear at this stage, because there is much debate about the extent of delocalisation, what is clear is that the auto industry is in the midst of the most radical restructuring since the war. By and large the restructuring process is being driven by new global trends (like the advent of Japanese transplants setting new benchmarks of performance) and new local circumstances (the fact that some established auto locations are no longer as competitive as they were).

The current restructuring of the European auto industry raises major questions not just about industrial adjustment at the sectoral level but, equally important, about social and economic regeneration at the regional level.

These two levels - the sectoral and the regional - have become more and more intermeshed in debates about the future of the auto industry. One of the main reasons for this intermeshing lies in the diffusion of the 'lean production model' which, among other things, sets a high premium on integrated supply chains (because close buyer-supplier relations are deemed to be essential to successful technology transfer, faster product development and higher quality standards). A key question here concerns the spatial impact of integrated supply chains, an issue which has spawned two schools of thought:

- on one side we have the argument that the trend towards integrated supply chains, with their emphasis on just-in-time delivery methods, is leading to a new process of spatial clustering because suppliers will be required to locate physically close to their major customers

- on the other side we have the argument that what matters most in a JIT- style environment is not clustering but a reliable, and therefore predictable, delivery pipeline, which means that suppliers can be located anywhere so long as they have access to a robust logistical system

While there is certainly some evidence to sustain the clustering effect (like BMW in Regensburg, Nissan in Sunderland and Fiat in Melfi for example) it seems that this thesis may have been exaggerated. Besides, can clustering coexist with the trend towards global sourcing? I raise these questions because the spatial consequences of integrated supply chains are decidedly unclear. However, this remains an important issue because the future viability of the European auto industry will depend on the integrity of the links between manufacturers and suppliers. Let us turn to consider the wider restructuring process in a core auto region.

2. Core Regions Under Duress: The Position of Baden-Wurttemberg

The traditional auto centres in Europe will not survive in their present form. All the manufacturers are frantically trying to cut their costs, reform their working practices and re-define their sourcing relationships so as to meet the Japanese challenge. Because greenfield locations make it easier to start anew, some firms are using greenfield sites to introduce radically new working practices. Perhaps the best example of this trend is Fiat, which is running down employment at its traditional sites (Turin and Milan) and setting new standards for itself at its greenfield plant at Melfi (in the southern region of Basilicata), where Fiat wants its primary suppliers to locate as well.

Paradoxically, perhaps, the auto centres which face the stiffest challenge are in Germany, the dominant player in the European auto industry. Germany alone accounts for 37% of West European car production and for 47% of the output of Europe's independent auto components industry. In August 1993 the VDA motor industry association said that the German auto industry would have to shed at least 100,000 jobs (from a workforce which then stood at over 690,000) and cut costs by between 20-30% by 1995 if it was to remain internationally competitive.

In terms of a number of different indicators - productivity, labour costs, working hours and absenteeism - the German auto industry appears to have fallen behind its key competitors in the past six years. On labour costs for example, the total hourly wage cost in Germany was DM49.62 in 1993, almost double the UK level of DM25.56.

These differentials help to explain the new-found fervour to accelerate the restructuring process in companies such as VW and Mercedes, whose main plants at Wolfsburg (Lower Saxony) and Sindelfingen (Baden-Wurttemberg) are thought to be especially uncompetitive. It also helps to explain the high premium which the German firms are now placing on foreign investment (e.g. BMW in the US and the UK, Mercedes in the

US and Spain) and outsourcing (which is designed to reduce costs by lowering the share of the car which is built in-house). In principle the trend towards greater outsourcing ought to mean more business for local German suppliers. In practice, however, the lion's share of this business appears to be going to lower cost locations outside Germany.

Acute as they are, the problems of large manufacturers like VW and Mercedes pale by comparison with the emerging crisis in the German components industry. This industry (which consists of some 3,000 firms, most of which are medium-sized companies) is one of the traditional bastions of the German Mittelstand, the backbone of the German economy. According to a sombre analysis from Price Waterhouse it is thought that, of this total, just 500 suppliers will emerge in a viable shape from the current restructuring gale. And, of these, Price Waterhouse expects around 100 to become first-tier suppliers, providing their customers with complete sub-assemblies. The current crisis of the Mittelstand firms comes hard on the heels of a growing financial squeeze. For example:

-   German vehicle prices rose by 26% between 1985-1992, while component prices increased by just 11% over the same period

-   the average return on sales in the German components sector fell from more than 5% in 1987 to just 1.5% in 1991

The challenge facing the European auto sector today is all too evident in Baden-Wurttemberg, one of Germany's premier auto centres and a region with a traditionally strong Mittelstand sector. As always, the most palpable sign of the crisis is on the labour front, where some 30,000 jobs disappeared between 1990-93, a trend which shows no sign of tapering off.

The auto industry in Baden-Wurttemberg developed in the form of a classic regional cluster (i.e. buyer-supplier linkages were deeply embedded and highly localised). A source of strength when the industry was buoyant, this regional cluster becomes part of the problem in the context of retrenchment - a sober reminder of the downside of the clustering process which is advocated in many quarters today. What seems to be happening is that this auto cluster is being hollowed out as the larger firms make greater use of single sourcing, which replaces several suppliers with one or two, and global sourcing, which substitutes global for local linkages.

In other words, de-localisation is taking two forms: on the one hand large firms like Mercedes and Bosch are building new plants outside Germany while, on the other hand, they are reducing the level of local sourcing from their existing plants. Taken together, these two trends represent a major crisis for many firms in the local auto components industry, a sector which is likely to become much more concentrated as a result of this restructuring process.

If these are some of the main elements of the problem, how can the restructuring process be managed at the regional level? At least two dimensions of the auto crisis have to be addressed as a matter of urgency. First, how to promote more cost-effective, more innovative and more integrated buyer-supplier linkages (the vertical networking challenge). Second, how to secure more cost-effective, more innovative and more collaborative R&D practices among the Mittelstand firms themselves (the horizontal networking challenge).

To facilitate the process of change the regional government has launched a "common initiative" for the region's auto industry, the aim being to bring together all the key players - leading firms, industry associations, chambers of commerce, unions, research institutes, etc. - so as to design a commonly agreed renewal strategy. To complement this initiative the government has announced a number of new 'flanking' measures, including:

-   the formation of expert groups under the auspices of the Ministry of Economics; among other things these groups will examine new avenues for inter-firm co-operation between large and small firms on the one hand and within the Mittel-stand sector on the other

-   a qualifications offensive to raise the level of both vocational and specialist skills

-   a more focused technology policy which seeks to tap the expertise of such key intermediaries as the Fraunhofer Institutes and the Steinbeis technology transfer centres so as to encourage closer partnerships between industry and research and to promote Baden-Wurttemberg as an 'ecological model region'

While better inter-firm collaboration is one of the keys to regional renewal, this strategy will have to surmount some serious obstacles. For example, large firms are perceived to be paying homage to 'vertical partnerships' with their suppliers at the same time as they squeeze the latter ever more tightly. Within the Mittelstand sector one of the main obstacles to closer inter-firm collaboration is the fierce sense of independence which has always been the hallmark of these family-run firms.

For all the gloom that pervades Baden-Wurttemberg today, there is also hope.

With a technical and training infrastructure that is second to none, this region seems well equipped to adjust to the 'lean production' era. Equally significant, the networking ethos - the disposition to collaborate to achieve mutually beneficial ends - continues to run deep, despite the obstacles. When the current restructuring storm is over, however, we will probably find that the simpler forms of production have migrated to lower cost locations outside the region, leaving behind a rather different regional cluster, with its main emphasis on the highly skilled activities of research, design, development and systems integration. This scenario may solve the problems of the stronger firms in the region, but it is of little comfort to the swollen ranks of unemployed auto workers in and around Stuttgart.

3. Prospects For The Peripheral Regions: The Position of Wales

Conventional wisdom suggests that the problems of the high cost core regions offer new opportunities for the low cost peripheral regions. If there is any truth in this view it is a partial truth because low cost per se is not a sufficient condition in an era of permanent innovation and exacting quality standards. Time was when low cost was thought to be synonymous with low quality, an equation which no longer holds true in countries like the UK, where the Japanese transplants have done much to raise the level of quality through their formidable vendor-building programmes. A combination of improved quality and low costs has made the UK an attractive location, especially from a sourcing standpoint. Indeed, VW, Mercedes and BMW are all stepping up their UK sourcing because it is felt that major savings - possibly up to 40% - can be achieved in this way. Proximity to the Japanese transplants reinforces the UK's attraction as an auto location because, by 1995, the combined UK purchasing of Nissan, Honda and Toyota is expected to be around £1.3 billion per annum.

This is the context in which Wales is emerging as a new regional base for the auto industry. While there are no final assembly plants in Wales, there is a vibrant automotive components sector composed of some 150 firms employing around 20,000 people, with a customer base that includes all the major car manufacturers. This sector has grown markedly in recent years, so much so that there is a greater concentration of automotive manufacturing in Wales (8.4% of total manufacturing employment) than in the UK as a whole (5.4%). The top end of the sector consists of leading names like Bosch, Valeo, Toyota, Teves, Ford and Calsonic, while the lower end consists of a more numerous group of indigenous small and medium-sized enterprises (SMEs).

While the Welsh auto sector conforms in many ways to a "branch-plant economy", this is no longer wholly synonymous with routine assembly functions because a process of upgrading appears to be underway. One index of this is the growth of professional engineers, scientists and technologists, a category which grew by 547% in Wales between 1978-90, compared to a decline of 1.3% in the UK as a whole. A recent survey found other encouraging signs, like the fact that 38% of firms reported increased R&D investment over the last 5 years; 71% operated along just-in-time lines; 45% had been awarded the BS5750 quality badge; 48% had achieved Ford's Q1 or Q101 standard; and 66% had initiated their own supplier development programmes.

The development of the auto sector has been actively promoted by the Welsh Development Agency (WDA), one of the most innovative regional development agencies in Europe. To promote Wales as an inward investment location the WDA has, until recently, relied upon low labour costs as the key attraction. This proved to be a decisive factor in persuading Bosch to locate its advanced alternator plant in South Wales, where total labour costs are 50% lower than in Stuttgart when measured in terms of personnel cost per hour worked.

Even in the European periphery, however, low labour costs are no longer a sufficient guarantee of success. Consequently, over the past two years, the WDA has been the key animator in diffusing best-practice manufacturing techniques throughout the sector. To this end it set up the Welsh Automotive Components Association, a sectoral self-help group in which large and small firms alike share the latest thinking and devise joint solutions to common problems. Equally significant, the WDA has helped to form training consortia for SMEs in the auto sector. By acting in concert these firms are able to reap two benefits: they are able to reduce the cost of training provision and they have been able to persuade local training providers to improve the quality of training provision.

Raising the calibre of these indigenous SMEs is rightly perceived to be an essential step, without which they will fail to meet the exacting quality standards of the larger auto customers. To nurture this upgrading process the WDA now offers a wide array of sophisticated technical assistance as part of its Supplier Development Programme, which has been well received by both the SMEs and the larger branch-plants in the region. What this experience shows is that some peripheral regions are not content to rely on low labour costs as the only source of competitive advantage in the 1990s.

4. Alleviating Regional Upheaval: A Modest Agenda

To speak of a coming crisis in Europe's auto-dependent regions is not an exaggeration. The clearest expression of this crisis will be on the labour front where, according to the Boston Consulting Group for example, more than 400,000 jobs are likely to be lost in the components sector alone before the end of the century. To alleviate the upheaval urgent and concerted action will be necessary at a number of different levels, especially at the supra-national and regional levels.

At the European level the problem would seem to be sufficiently acute to justify a Konver-like programme for the auto industry. This could complement the horizontal policy measures which the Commission plans to introduce under the new Objective 4, the aim of which is to anticipate the consequences of industrial change on workers in employment and to address future skill needs with special emphasis on SMEs. As necessary as they are, these short term fire-fighting measures are no substitute for a sound, longer term response.

The challenge facing the auto industry today is a microcosm of the wider challenge to the European economy, where the key problem is the knowledge-transfer problem. Very simply, this consists of Europe's poor record in converting scientific and technological knowledge into commercially successful products and services, the inability to transfer knowledge from laboratory to industry and from firm to firm. At bottom, Europe lacks a robust networking culture, that is the disposition to collaborate to achieve mutually beneficial ends. Applying this to the auto industry we can say that without new and more innovative forms of networking, this industry will not be able to meet the challenge ahead, a challenge which consists of radically improved methods of designing, developing and producing cars, the growing use of new materials and advanced electronics, more exacting safety and environmental standards and the requirement to interact with 'intelligent' road and transport infrastructures.

To help meet this challenge - which is beyond the reach of any single firm working in isolation - the Commission should aim to promote a stronger networking culture if the full potential of the RTD effort is to be realised. Given the need for a concerted approach there ought to be much more horizontal integration between the Commission's own activities, especially as between the Framework Programme and the Structural Funds, and this requires stronger interfaces between DGs III, XII, XVI and XXIII in particular.

Turning to the regional dimension it is now generally accepted that this is the most appropriate level at which to deploy innovation support programmes, not just for SMEs but for large branch-plants as well. Access to a technology transfer system that is attuned to local needs, yet receptive to cross-border opportunities, is one of the most important ingredients in the recipe for regional renewal. If firms are to remain viable players in the auto industry, or if they wish to diversify into related product markets, they will need local access to technical support and re- training facilities. Building a more robust institutional capacity at local and regional levels is perhaps the most pressing issue of all if these areas are going to be able to regenerate themselves. After all, no amount of external support, whether from central government or the Commission, can ever substitute for the lack of an endogenous dynamic within each region. To nurture this dynamic the principle of subsidiarity, which stresses the devolution of decision-making competence, ought to be applied more forcefully, especially in countries like the UK, where it is perceived to be confined to the national level.

For their part the regions most affected by auto industry restructuring will need to exchange ideas and share experiences with respect to best-practice local economic development strategies. To its credit MILAN (the Motor Industry Local Authority Network) has played an important role here in brokering exchanges between auto locales throughout the Europe.

Finally, perhaps the key point to make is for us to recognise industrial innovation and regional development for what they really are, namely collective social endeavours. What this means is that inter-dependence - between management and labour within the firm, between firms in the supply chain and between companies and their local milieux - needs to be more consciously acknowledged and more actively developed. If this can be done Europe will be on the way to creating a stronger networking culture and this, in turn, is the basis for more innovative models of corporate and regional development.

Thank you for listening.

Mr Mihr:

Thank you Professor Morgan. Now I should like to turn to the European Commission, to the recent paper on the European Automobile Industry. We have today Mr Dufeil of the Directorate General for Regional Policy.

📖 *Mr Dufeil:*

Thank you Mr Mihr. Mr Landaburu cannot be here to day, and has asked me to speak to this Forum on his behalf.

European Union policy with regard to adaptation

How can the Structural Funds complement the efforts which both the automobile manufacturers and the components manufacturers are being required to make in the field of adaptation, and how can the latter contribute, for their part, in promoting a policy of cohesion?

We should begin by pointing out that, by their very nature, Structural Fund contributions are horizontal, i.e., they do not involve specific sectoral measures. Up to a point, however, Structural Fund contributions can still provide benefits for the automobile sector on the basis of the priorities to be adopted by common agreement between the Commission and the Member States.

It should also be recalled that the Structural Funds have a key role to play in facilitating the structural changes and, pursuant to Articles 123 and 127 of the Treaty, in drawing up measures to facilitate the adaption of workers to industrial changes and to changes in production systems, in particular through vocational training and retraining. There is a clear link between this approach and the approach adopted under Article 30, involving steps to "ensure that the conditions necessary for the competitiveness of the Community's industry exist". In point of fact, the aim of these measures is twofold: to improve the competitiveness of the undertakings and, at the same time, to avoid job losses. During the new planning period (1994-99), therefore, the Structural Funds will devote particular attention, irrespective of region, to the development of human resources.

Let us now briefly run through the intervention measures that have special relevance to the automobile industry in this context.

1. The new objective No 4 pursued under the Structural Funds with a view to promoting the adaption of the labour force to structural changes. The grants awarded in the form of Community support outside the regions indicated in Objective No 1, in which are located most of the vehicle and spare-part production units, amount to more than 2 MECU for the period 1994-99. The aim of this horizontal training instrument is to anticipate the effects of industrial change and changes in production systems on workers engaged in active employment. It will also cover future skilled-labour needs by placing special emphasis on SMEs. Leaving this priority aside, the combined efforts of the manufacturers and suppliers in the field of co-operation could prove particularly significant in attracting potential assistance measures. It is now up to the Member States to accord priorities to the possibilities opened up by this new objective and to ensure that the implementing programmes are characterised by a high degree of attention to detail.

2. The second intervention mechanism concerns the new ADAPT Community initiative, which will supplement the measures set out in Objective No 4 to which I

have just referred, notably through co-operation measures across the entire Community. The amount allocated to this initiative has been fixed at 1,400 MECU, including 1,000 MECU to be devoted to the regions located outside the zones indicated in Objective No 1. The initiative seeks, on the one hand, to promote partnership and co-operation among the undertakings, research centres, training bodies and public authorities and, on the other, to develop networks and co-operation involving the manufacturers, suppliers and consumers, including both large-scale manufacturers and suppliers and small and medium-sized enterprises.

The feature which gives the ADAPT initiative its special character is its "bottom-up" approach, whereby the industry, management and labour and the regions are all involved in determining priorities and preparing the measures arising therefrom. As a matter of priority, these measures will be multisectoral, transnational or inter-regional in character.

3. The third intervention mechanism concerns the new Community initiative to promote SMEs (1,000 MECU) by providing opportunities to strengthen the latter's capacity for action in the context of an integrated approach. The sum of 200 MECU has been allocated to regions not covered by Objective No 1 (i.e., 2 and 5b).

This initiative includes measures which seek to stimulate investment through the acquisition of know-how and of better organizational and technological capabilities. In this way it will be possible to assist the SMEs in adapting to the changing roles of the subcontractors and large enterprises, in particular.

In the interests of efficiency, it will be necessary to focus this initiative on the following restricted range of priority topics:

- improving the production systems and SME organizational structures, primarily through physical investment linked to the adoption of a total quality strategy, the promotion of technological innovations and the management, organization and use of modern communications and information systems;

- taking account of the environment and the rational use of energy;

- encouraging co-operation between the research centres and the SMEs in the area of technology transfer and applications so as to encourage the SMEs to pursue innovation and take on highly qualified personnel;

- facilitating access to new contracts, including public procurement contracts within the Single Market as well as third-country markets;

- developing co-operation between the research centres and the SMEs in the area of technology transfer and applications so as to encourage the SMEs to pursue innovation and take on highly qualified personnel;

- strengthening professional qualifications within the SMEs in the light of these priority topics. You will note that these two initiatives (ADAPT and SME) stem directly from the ideas set out in the White Paper on Growth, Competitiveness and Employment.

4. Lastly, let us recall the traditional forms of intervention associated with the Structural Funds: productive investment and infrastructure investment, notably in the roads sector. Since 1993 this category of infrastructure has also benefited from additional resources provided under the new Cohesion Fund targeted on the four least prosperous countries of the Union: Greece, Spain, Portugal and Ireland. Let us also recall the significant role played by the EIB through the granting of loans for the creation of road infrastructures.

Although not exhaustive, this table of Community structural intervention mechanisms highlights the essential aspects making up a potential focus of attention for the Community automobile industry.

It is true that the resources administered by the Structural Funds are allocated, as a matter of priority, to the regions in greatest need, i.e., those regions lagging behind in terms of the implementation of Objective No. 1. This is something that is stipulated under Fund rules and which, it seems to me, is fully justified.

The Commission is also aware that, in contrast to the location of the traditional conversion sectors, the bulk of the activity (and hence employment) in the automobile sector is located in the FEDER intervention regions.

On the one hand, however, certain changes have already taken place in the distribution patterns governing the location of the automobile industry, as a result of the relocation trends affecting the sector. In, fact we have established that a number of new investments have been allocated to the peripheral regions (i.e., the former GDR (Opel/VW), Mezzogiorno (Fiat), Portugal (VW/Ford) and Spain (several manufacturers). (Some of these investments, moreover, have benefited from support from the ERDF and the ESF.)

There can be no denying that this has had beneficial effects from the point of view of cohesion. Apart from the direct impact on employment, there have also been indirect effects involving technology transfers, know-how and new prospects for local suppliers.

On the other hand, this also explains why it is proper that Structural Fund intervention mechanisms should prompt manufacturers to think in terms of cohesion, when drawing up their development plans.

However, to conclude from the foregoing that, henceforth, only specialised activities offering high added value and of a technological nature will remain in the central regions would be premature and unrealistic.

The likely outcome - because of the concentration of the automobile industry in certain prosperous regions - is that those regions, in particular, may be faced with social and economic challenges, arising from the restructuring, of a kind that they have not hitherto been required to cope with.

Attempting to quantify the regional repercussions of the structural adjustments, notably in the field of employment, is no simple matter. Indeed, the unknown parameters in this area are legion. Nevertheless, the regional effects are certain to be largely determined by the changing relations between manufacturers and suppliers and the resulting structural adjustments.

At all events, the Commission will monitor these trends closely, particularly as regards their regional impact in the field of employment.

Nor can it be ruled out that the socio-economic situation in certain central regions, where the automobile sector is concentrated in force, may deteriorate to such an extent as to warrant special consideration being given to these problems by the Structural Funds at some future date. We shall be taking these factors into account in 1996-97, in particular, when the list of regions covered by Objective No 2, c and d, come up for review.

Mr Mihr:

Thank you Mr Dufeil. In no way were you a mere substitute for your Director General - you made an excellent presentation. Thank you very much.

Now I would like to introduce Mr Adelt, a member of the board of Volkswagen AG, with responsibility for financial matters. A spectacular agreement was reached a few weeks ago: an entirely new approach was adopted, and this at a time of crisis, with mass redundancies in areas such as Brunswick in Germany being a major threat - and so the route taken was most interesting.

▢ *Mr Adelt:*

Thank you. First let me apologise on behalf of Mr Hartz, who was not able to be present today. He is the author of this presentation, and it is an honour for me to be here in his place.

As has been said several times, there is a structural crisis facing the European automobile industry, and we see no end to this at the moment.

Concretely, for Volkswagen, this means that both existing progress in productivity should be harnessed to catch up with and overtake the Japanese and the Americans, as well as to compensate for the enormous fall in demand for cars of last year. This challenge, if met with only traditional means, would imply the dismissal of almost 30,000 workers in Volkswagen this year. These jobs would be lost almost entirely in Lower Saxony, one of the regions of the world most dependent on the automobile industry.

In the US, 0.8 % of the industrial workforce works in the automobile sector. In Japan the figure is 1.3 %, and in Western Germany it is greater than 3 %. In Lower Saxony the figure is almost 6 %. Almost a quarter of the financial turnover of the region of Lower Saxony is achieved by Volkswagen. So if 30,000 redundancies had occurred in Lower Saxony, there would have been a disastrous situation economically and socially. New routes had to be found towards reducing costs significantly whilst at the same time maintaining the workers' jobs with appropriate increases in productivity.

In just 15 months, almost 38,000 jobs were adjusted. This represented a third of the 120,000 people we were employing in VW, and this was achieved without any individual dismissals, or any industrial disputes. About 18,000 people took early retirement, and a further 20,000 jobs went using various creative methods. People have remained employed by Volkswagen; they will not go on the dole in Lower Saxony. New work systems will enable a further 10,000 working relationships to be dismantled.

So this is another push beyond classical working methods, and the four-day week. We hope to make a number of savings on the work side, some DM 3.5 billion, and a number of endeavours should increase this potential. Overall competitiveness will be increased.

Since the beginning of the year the 28.8 hour working week has come into effect at VW, i.e. 20 % less than before. We remain free and flexible, and able to adapt upwards if demand were to increase suddenly, or downwards if demand were to decline further. In some areas, for example in research and development, the 28.8 hour week requires enormous creativity and flexibility, and this is difficult to achieve. We have specific working time models to meet this need, which we have developed to implement this 28.8 hour working week. Imbalances remain in terms of personnel capacity. We seek to make up for these in transfers and in retraining. Our additional relay and block-time models have given us a breathing space, and are allowing us to adjust the employment level further downwards.

We have agreed on a sort of relay model. Younger people will enter into an increasing working relationship. Over a period of 42 months, worktime will increase progressively from 18 to 28.8 hours a week. Older workers will reduce their working hours, possibly from the age of 50, but more desirably from the age of 56. So they will be passing the bat on to younger people, on a flexible basis. This should enable 10,000 jobs based on a 4-day week and flexible working hours to be created.

To improve skills, we offer block times. Workers can interrupt their work for four to six months, in order to prepare for a later period through intensive training. The block model makes it possible to adapt the pattern of employment to the labour market. The variability and flexibility of employment should be cover everything. Days, weeks, the seasons and every aspect of working life are all taken into account. We require variability in order to keep more people in employment in ways which are acceptable. In order to take this approach, and to manage change, we need to take on people who are more broadly and more fully qualified, and who can be used more fully internationally. We need people who can steer the adaptation process creatively, and act responsibly socially. We require workers who are ready to accept new forms of contracts of employment. Volkswagen will remain the rule for a good, long-term working relationship, but as a good quid pro quo, people have to accept more flexibility and mobility than in the past. We need an instrument for peak work and structural change, something which is not removed and hopelessly alienated from the new workplace.

The coaching company is supposed to bring about training with this end in mind, and it is supposed to undertake development in Lower Saxony. This example can serve as a model for the rest of Europe, and will serve as a pilot for the rest of our industry. The coaching company has two main tasks. To tackle the regional structural problems of the automobile industry in the region of Lower Saxony, and to implement the most innovative personnel concepts.

We are living through a structural crisis at the moment, and we should be ready, instead of shifting the burden of finding solutions to our problems onto others, to do something about it ourselves. We have to see what we can contribute which is acceptable, a new form of acceptability, which is the key to applying new forms of solutions. I think we have achieved this in Volkswagen with everyone accepting burdens, without exception, with those at the bottom of the hierarchy making the smallest sacrifices. We have managed to achieve a lot in a short time, and we are happy that our negotiating partners, the Unions and the labour representation boards, have been happy to go along with us in this way. This is a sign of change that we want to utilise. We want to be able to break new ground. European industry requires employment models such as this which can enhance competitiveness, not bring it down. This will stabilise the labour market, and will sustain prospects for workers. Industry has done what it had to do in the past, and will continue to do so. The Volkswagen model is just one example from European industry. Without the assistance of the public authorities, structural change will not be mastered. To create new jobs for the 21st century, public authorities will have to assist.

I'm pleased that this Forum has been set up for the Commission to explain how it is going to implement its ambitious aims.

Thank you.

Mr Mihr:

Thank you for that presentation Mr Adelt.

Ladies and gentlemen, I don't think it is a secret that this sort of thing affects our regions, such as Volkswagen in Lower Saxony for example, which has been more than welcomed by people in political authority and in public opinion in Germany, and I can only call upon people to look very hard at this model, rather than just disregarding it from the outset.

Now, as the last main speaker I would like to introduce the Mayor of Barcelona, as obviously since our subject today has such an important effect regionally, leaders of city public authorities have some very important things to say.

Mr Maragall:

I will make ten short points.

I think one has to divide the situation of the automobile industry in Europe into two types of zone. Those with a tradition in the manufacturing industry, and those where investment in the manufacturing industry is more recent. In the second case the impact of the present crisis is much much stronger than in the first. This is the first point. In Spain we have a network called RECA, the Spanish network of automobile-producing cities. We see this very clearly, this difference between some areas and others.

The second point I should like to make concerns the internationalisation of our industries. This may be beneficial in the medium term, but it is not good in the short term because it causes some problems in terms of employment.

Third point: Competitivity means more and more investment in just-in-time techniques. This environment does have a lot do with the type of industry we have producing components for the industry. There has been a dramatic reduction in the number of components produced for automobiles, and a dramatic narrowing of the space left for the traditional auxiliary industry.

Fourth point: The situation represents one area of conflict in the inter-regional arena, a very strong one. A solution has to be found which cannot cease to be really effective in crisis situations. We have to find solutions for jobs which go beyond this industry.

Fifth point: If we are to minimise the impact of the crisis, we have to bring imagination into the scenario. Another way out. We can make some use of the redundant space left by the automobile industry. We can also push forward the line of the urban ecological vehicle. I am one of those who believes that in the future, as well as the distinction between car and truck, we are going to learn to distinguish between urban car and road car.

Sixth point. Another traditional alternative has been the conversion of staff, opening space to a sector of services, and especially those of low qualification. There are some difficulties with that, but one must not forget the fact that tourism in general, and urban tourism in particular, are alternatives.

We speak only about the recuperation of a number of jobs and only some 25-35 % of those which have been lost. With the kind of solutions I've been talking about, we've only been aiming at a small part of the employment which has been lost. So we have to take up a double strategy in depth. On the one hand it must be based on the real perspective of the sectoral limits of the crisis, and to make use of the possible, likely, change of sign of the economic cycle, to create conditions for an alternative industrial policy which includes the recycling of personnel.

Eighth point: We have to aid the reconversion of the affected regions, but this has to be done through cross-fertilisation systems, which combine investment policies along with technological processes. The zones where the decision to install automobile industries was due to the attraction of cheap manpower are suffering much more than are the other ones.

Tenth point. I said I'd only make ten points. Well I've got thirteen in mind now, but I'll stop there. Tenth point: The combination of industry services has to be kept up in cities. Cities provide a climate of social and economic re-equilibrium.

Eleven.   Vocational training and research are absolutely prime issues.   Neither national resources nor capital are going to be as crucial as professional know-how. Our professional training and university systems are going to be decisive here.

Twelve: Political powers have to increase their co-operation with the private sector. We in Barcelona, as you probably know, have nowadays a problem of adaptation in the Seat-Volkswagen plant in the free zone, and I am glad to announce, as the President of a small but very active risk-capital-raising company, in which both regional and city government hold shares, that we are eager and ready to co-operate along with private companies in order to create the environment necessary to overcome this crisis. I should add that we are the owners of the land in which this factory is located, which is another incentive for us to get in, but even if this were not the case, we would be in there anyway. We have a very positive attitude, not in the sense of just building a lot of buildings, which is not the case, but in implementing all the instruments we have in our power in order to overcome this crisis - and it will be overcome. Barcelona City Council is prepared to intervene and to help Seat-Volkswagen in the creation of a suppliers park, as they call it, close to the old Volkswagen-Seat factory in the free zone of Barcelona.

I also want to announce that in June, June 22-23, Barcelona has been asked to organise a Euro-Conference, for European firms and European enterprises, which will have only three items on the agenda: the first is cars; the second cable, the third is recycling. At this meeting, heads of industry will be telling Mayors how they want the streets to be, and we will be telling them how we want cars to be. I don't think there is another real way out, other than sitting down together and telling one another what we would like the other to have done by the year 2000.

That is my last point, my thirteenth I regret to say, that cities have to contribute from a strategic point of view, beyond the tactical urgencies of the moment, and get together the economic and social groupings who have an interest here, the industries, the Unions, the Universities and the like. Through the elaboration of strategic plans, which will define the sectors where one should act, and which would design policies for the cities of the future.

Thank you.

Mr Mihr:

Thank you very much, Mr Mayor. I expect that the representatives of industry have heard the message that industry should stay in the city.

I would like to turn to Dr Camerana, who is the Deputy Chairman of the Board of Magneti Marelli, the component suppliers. You have the floor, sir.

📖 ***Dr Camerana:***

I want to give you some information on managing the structural changes.

At the end of the 1980s, we were facing the requirements of the car manufacturers. We all know that they were going through much tougher competition, which could only mean reduction in prices for us, the component manufacturers.

On the other hand, we understood that the trend would go from multiple local sourcing towards global single sourcing, or maybe double sourcing. On the other hand, as far as components manufacturers were concerned, we understood that the car manufacturers would privilege the integration from single component into multiple component manufacturers, meaning subsystem manufacturers, and that required massive investments in electronics.

Finally, we also understood that the car manufacturers needed us to be able to migrate from other areas where the car manufacturers would establish themselves. Being small companies ourselves, we understood that we had to grow into larger companies, and that we could only do so through alliances, mergers and through acquisitions. Perhaps many other companies should do the same things. These rationalisations, these alliances, had to be based on the availability of know-how and of technology aimed at innovative subsistence. Also, very importantly, financing new resources for the newly formed alliances and joint ventures. As far as cost reductions are concerned, we had to move into innovative product development, because cost is essentially dependent on the design of the product. We needed highly flexible manufacturing facilities, and this means lean production. We also needed applied geographical positioning, to be able to be near the development centres of the car manufacturers, and also to be able to establish multi-customer relationships, and this means logistics.

These were the basic challenges we were facing. Very simply, I am going to tell you what we did between 1986 and 1993. We merged with and acquired a number of companies. We assembled two companies in the electromechanics field, ourselves and Lucas Starters and Alternators. We merged two companies in the carburettors area, Weber and Solex in France and Italy. In the lighting business, three companies, two in Italy and one in the UK, Lucas. In France and in Italy, in instrumentation. This is what we did to start with, we merged and put together these companies. After that we began a rationalisation programme regarding these companies. Rationalising the number of plants, lowering the break-even point, setting up innovative managerial and teamwork instruments. We also began developing new business, mainly in electronics. Electronics, as we have heard repeatedly today, are fundamental to automotive components. We entered into the fuel injection business. We were leaders in the field of carburettors, which have now practically disappeared, and so we had to invest in fuel injection.

On the other hand, we've rejected some areas which we did not consider strategically suitable, such as wire harnesses, since we only had one customer there. Diesel pumps and injectors for the same reason. Batteries because we were mainly located in Italy. We had to enter into a very high level of technical and managerial training. All of our people who had different origins had to feel like they were members of one single company.

So, in 1993 we have achieved the objectives we set out with. We had, in 1987, 75 sites in Europe. We now have 31. Our sales have increased fourfold, to over ECU 4 billion. In research and development, and in investment in new technologies, in other words our resources spent on the future, represent 14 % of our sales.

Our personnel was virtually 100 % in Italy. Now that level has come down to 45 %, with 20 % in France, 35 % in the rest of Europe, i.e. Spain, UK, Turkey and Poland, and about 15 % in North and South America.

Our sales were 75 % in Italy, in 1986. Now only 28 % of our sales are to Italian car manufacturers, 25 to French, 15 to German and others.

As far as our product portfolio is concerned, we have reduced it to only a few, being leader or second in the market. In fuel injection we consider ourselves number two, starters and alternators number three, in the instruments cluster I think we are number one in Europe. In headlights and taillights we are number two in Europe. We have rationalised our product line too.

This is just to give you an idea of what we have done. We have been inspired by the customer satisfaction philosophy. We have achieved in this period a rationalisation and a development project, positioning ourselves first in Europe, and being ready to support our customers whenever they want to move to an emerging market, such as Poland, Turkey, China, whatever.

All of this has represented a very great managerial effort, and I think that similar efforts should be made by other companies in the components field, and I think the political authorities of the European Union should consider that these rationalisation programmes, which are needed, require some financing from the EC.

Thank you.

Mr Mihr:

Thank you Dr Camerana. I would now like to introduce my colleague from the European Parliament, Ms Brigitte Ernst de la Graete. Ms Ernst de la Graete, you have the floor.

Ms Ernst de la Graete:

Thank you very much Mr Chairman. I shall not speak at length.

Given that in the Economic and Monetary Affairs Committee I was the author of a report on the links between industry and the environment, I would like to say a few things on this subject.

The first point I'd like to make is that I have the feeling that the automobile industry has not responded dynamically enough as yet to the challenges posed by global climate changes, and most particularly to the ambition that the Commission harboured of stabilising CO_2 emissions in the year 2000 at those of 1990. So, in that respect I think that the public authorities can use incentives, first working through research and development, and I do think that there are prospects emerging here at company level, that there also should be some efforts made at the European level, and secondly the idea of taxing energy and CO_2 as the Commission has proposed.

The second action which I see as necessary in the industry-environment context is the electric vehicle. This does not constitute a solution to all the problems, but you will understand that as representatives of those areas which are sensitive to environmental issues, we consider the electric car as being a mere shifting of pollution, instead of being an overall solution to the problem.

The third field of action is the durability of products, the durability of cars. Is this a solution or not? I think it should be examined, opening as it does opportunities for jobs in the fields of repairs and maintenance, the replacement of some parts, the adaptation of some new technical requirements for emission standards, of course. The other side of the coin is the problem of the renewal of the fleet, so that standards should be aligned more with the standards set at European level than it is at present. There is therefore here a tension between the durability of products and the need to adapt the car fleet to requirements in term of the environment and technological progress, and I think that there the Commission ought to formulate its own approach and state its position more clearly.

One further point: recycling. I think if one is to take seriously the vision of recycling of cars at the end of their lives, then I think it is necessary to look at this question of recycling at the time of design. I think the most acute problem is that of multi-material new components for which recycling poses major problems. I do think that here again the public authorities have to have a very clear view of the way in which the market has to be reorganised with a view to allowing the component parts of cars to be more completely recycled.

The last point on the environment which I should like to make is the promotion of public transport. I feel that this point is not dealt with sufficiently in the Commission's recent Communication. To count on an increase of registrations of new cars in the medium term is not very realistic, given the damage this can cause in terms of CO_2 in bottlenecks in cities, noise and in the saturation of the road network. We think there are considerable prospects in the development of efficient public transport, and that we shouldn't necessarily see this as a competitor to the automobile industry, but rather complementary to it. I think that new technology and components can bring about progress.

One last point on social problems. You have to realise that not very far from here in Forest there is a Volkswagen assembly plant, and I would like to ask the representative of Volkswagen who, luckily for us, is here today, about the rumour going about that soon this plant's role is going to be transferred to Asian partners, and that this will bring about job reductions and dismissals. What do you think of this? Do you think that transferring this production to a partner that has a different line of models in production than yours manifestly, certainly in terms of work policies, is a good solution? Is this part of the European model that you were recommending, or are you going to be able to deny and be able to reassure the employees at the site, who up to now have not been fully satisfied in this respect?

Thank you Mr Chairman.

Mr Mihr:

Thank you very much. The last speaker is Mr Firth, of the regional authority network MILAN.

Mr Firth:

The Motor Industry Local Authority Network (MILAN) speaks on behalf of local and regional authorities where the motor industry is located.

MILAN believes that local and regional authorities have a significant role to play in ensuring the health of Europe's motor industry, and of the communities that support it.

MILAN welcomes the establishment of this Forum.

Industrial restructuring, like that currently occurring in Europe's motor industry, has many consequences for regions and communities.

A global industry like the motor industry is still based upon local foundations, and is rooted in local communities. Local authorities are a key part of the local community in providing many of the resources (human, economic, physical) upon which the industry relies.

The existing activities of local and regional authorities should be fully incorporated into discussion of future policy at European level: for instance, in the areas of research and development, retraining, and social dialogue.

A new era of partnership in policy making requires that all relevant actors are included as "social partners", including local and regional authorities.

European policy should recognise and deal with the fact that in some regions, the motor industry no longer requires the human, economic and physical resources upon which it once relied and which came to depend upon it.

Programs that emphasise timely intervention to rechannel resources into productive uses will help prevent the onset of long-term economic decline which would be more costly in the long-term.

The Motor Industry Local Authority Network

The Motor Industry Local Authority Network (MILAN) represents 34 local authorities (county, city and district governments) in the United Kingdom where the motor industry plays a significant role in the local economy and the local community. MILAN represents the broad community interest in the motor industry: local citizens directly and indirectly involved in the industry, small and medium sized enterprises, and local authorities themselves. Local authorities are represented in MILAN by elected councillors, and each local authority makes a financial contribution towards MILAN research and development activities.

MILAN undertakes many activities. Each year it organises several visits to factories and companies to learn more about the changing motor industry. There are regular seminars for members to learn more about the industry and more about local policy making. A research programme is commissioned every year from expert university academics and expert consultants. MILAN reacts swiftly to unexpected events (such as the collapse of DAF/Leyland-Daf in 1993, news of the BMW purchase of Rover) by holding forums where local authorities can learn about and discuss the implications of these events for their local communities.

MILAN is actively involved in communicating with the UK national government. MILAN was recently invited to submit a statement, reflecting MILAN' s expertise in policy towards small and medium enterprises, to the House of Commons Select Committee on Trade and Industry."

MILAN and Europe

MILAN also participates in the European network of local authorities "Co-operation between Automobile Regions" (CAR), both to exchange innovative policy making experiences across Europe and to strengthen the local community voice at European Union level as far as the motor industry is concerned. Indeed MILAN members take a special interest in European Union policy and programs. This interest goes well beyond the "special pleading for a particular region" that some people associate with lobbying by local and regional authorities.

MILAN does not, therefore, seek merely to represent particular local authorities or particular regions in the United Kingdom. Rather, it tries to answer the questions: how can local and regional authorities across Europe best contribute to European Union policy discussions regarding the motor industry? What significant roles do local and regional authorities play in the healthy functioning of the European motor industry? How can European Union programs best build upon and utilise the skills, expertise, and resources of local and regional authorities?

In 1992 MILAN published a statement on European Community policy, in response to the Second Communication on the motor industry published by the European Commission, also in 1992. That MILAN statement is still valid, and it can be summarised as follows:

(i)   MILAN should be considered a social partner in European dialogue on the motor industry.

(ii) MILAN members are well acquainted with working at the intersection of horizontal and sectoral policy.

(iii) MILAN supports the direction of European Community policy as expressed in recent Communications issued by the European Commission.

(iv) The significant role played by local and regional authorities in Europe has not yet been fully integrated into Community policy making.

(v)   Local and regional authorities have an important role to play in design and delivery of policies towards:

a) research and development (at small and medium enterprises in particular);

b) training and retraining;

c) promoting social dialogue;

(vi) Explicit recognition and inclusion of local and regional authority activities would enable better policies to be designed and many policies to be executed more effectively.

The Forum on the European Automobile Industry provides a significant opportunity to engage in the kind of dialogue proposed in the above MILAN policy statement. MILAN members are pleased to be invited to the Forum, and welcome the fact that one of the workshops is devoted to "The Car Industry and the Regions: The Management of Change".

Changes in the Motor Industry: The Regional Dimension

Many regions and local communities, across Europe, are dependent upon motor industry activities. The industry is also scattered widely in other places where its role is less prominent but still significant. This last point is reflected in the widespread national coverage of MILAN members in the United Kingdom. The same point can be made for the majority of countries in Europe.

How are current changes in the motor industry affecting these regions and local communities? What role do these regions and local communities play in ensuring the health of the motor industry in Europe?

Industrial Restructuring, Regional Restructuring

There is little doubt that, from the global scale down to the local scale, the motor industry is currently engaged in extensive restructuring, involving:

-   new production methods

-   new ways of utilising labour forces new relationships between purchasers and vendors up and down the chain from research through production to sales

- new materials, new product development processes

- new concerns over quality and over environmental issues and

- new geographical patterns of production and employment

Our understanding of these changes is very important because it forms the basis of policy and strategy formation. Beside commissioning their own research, MILAN members have studied with great interest the recent report on the motor components sector produced by Boston Consulting Group.

Industrial restructuring is frequently accompanied by regional restructuring. It is possible to identify several change trends in the European motor industry that have significant implications for regional and local economies and communities. The following are only the most significant examples:

(i) Concentration of Capital Following Mergers and Takeovers

Newly merged companies possess a new set of factories and facilities, allowing and sometimes requiring significant reorganization of the use made of these sites from a corporate viewpoint.

(ii) Increased Competition between Plants within Companies

Management often, explicitly or implicitly, sets factories and facilities in competition with each other for new investments. By extension, localities and regions which rely upon these sites are forced to compete too.

(iii) Opening up Eastern Europe

Once expected to be an economic saviour for Western Europe, this turns out only to be so in a limited sense. Eastern Europe's "best use" from a company viewpoint seems to be as a low-cost production site. The opening of Eastern Europe has accelerated both trends identified above, leading to concentration of capital and inter-place competition on a vast European scale.

(iv) Overcapacity

This is a difficult topic that deserves more thorough treatment. Here we can only make the following points:

- the producers are generally very reticent to admit the existence of overcapacity

- responsible officials at the European Union still seem to prefer to ignore overcapacity

- the United States experience, however, is instructive: construction of new factories by Japanese and domestic firms during the 1980s was followed by a major wave of factory closures (General Motors especially), waiting in the wings for several years until ushered on-stage by recession

- factually speaking, the European and American owned companies are equally responsible for the building of excess capacity in Europe as are the new Japanese investors.

The big question from the regional and local viewpoint remains unanswered: how will the pattern of plant closures and production cutbacks be reflected geographically.? Not just who - firms, plants, workforces - wins, who loses, but where will the winners and losers be located? The patterns are likely to be uneven: in 1993 and 1994, for instance, some areas of Spain are experiencing difficult problems (SEAT, Nissan, Suzuki). Theoretically, some of Ford's factories could have to be closed during the 1990s, or some of Fiat's, to name but two examples.

(v) Restructuring Manufacturing Methods

Lean production, just-in-time, and all the changes to manufacturing organization and operations discussed by the Boston Consulting Group report: what is the most conducive local and regional environment in which to undertake these activities? Are some places better suited than others, for reasons of labour force, management culture, infrastructures, location of linked companies? How does just-in-time affect spatial structures? What do new tiering arrangements in the supplier chain mean for smaller companies? It is clear that the national and regional and local environment in which firms operate affects their competitiveness; social and political, physical, training, buyer-supplier relations, among other factors.

(vi) European Union Policy

European Union policy is one of the contextual factors affecting the operations of the motor industry, and its regional and local activities. This includes: efforts to devise a strategy to help restructure the sector to boost competitiveness, led by DG III of the European Commission; negotiations with Japan over Japanese exports which may, or may not, include an understanding on the role of Japanese "transplants" in Europe, led by DG I; the very significant DG IV Framework for State Aid to the Motor Industry, which is setting strict limits on both national and local support programs for the sector in the hope of "levelling the playing field" and severely restricting big subsidies to attract new investments or retain old ones. The activities of other branches of the European Union also affect the motor industry's activities in ways which may affect its regional impacts. The particular concern in the European Parliament over the environmental impact of motor vehicles can be cited.

Local roots of a global industry

In discussions over industrial changes that focus on global and international trends, it is not unusual for the local and regional level to be ignored. Yet the roots, the foundations, upon which a healthy industry is built, are to be found at this level.

Even the most global of industries, the most multinational of companies, builds its operations upon local and regional foundations. The local activities of a company, and therefore its relationship to its immediate regional environment, play a very significant role in the health of a company. Here we refer to:

- physical infrastructures (transport, telecommunications)

- skilled work-force (education, training)

- local linkages with other companies (suppliers, purchasers)

It is essential not to neglect the foundations upon which those wider links are built. In MILAN's view, there remains a danger that the regional and local level is still being omitted or is being taken for granted in current discussions over future European Union policy towards the motor industry. There is some evidence of positive change in recent documents published by the European Commission and European Parliament, but progress can and should be accelerated.

As far as the relationship between the European motor industry and its local roots is concerned, there is in fact a double process taking place. Either the local and regional roots of the motor industry are being abandoned or cut back significantly (factory closures, large-scale loss of employment), or where they are maintained, the very nature of the relationship between industry and regional and local community is being altered.

(i) The continued health of an economic sector as a whole does not imply the health of the local and regional economies that have historically supported and nourished it. Indeed the health of a sector like the motor industry is frequently rebuilt via a restructuring process at the expense of existing workers and communities and a geographical shift of economic activities that can devastate whole communities.

(ii) Where substantial activity in a sector like the motor industry does remain in a particular region, major changes are called for. Many regions, across Europe, are dependent on motor industry activities. It should be recognized that those regions also make a substantial contribution towards the competitiveness of the European motor industry.

The particular input that MILAN can make to discussions over policy to aid the European motor industry lies in the unique viewpoint of local authorities. Although the precise situation differs from country to country in Europe, local authorities are usually responsible for maintaining and nurturing the local roots of the motor industry.

Equally important, it is the responsibility of MILAN members and other local authorities in European to ensure that any transition process away from the motor industry, whether for individual employees, small companies, or whole communities, takes place in a socially responsible way, a way which helps the communities to remain economically dynamic.

What should be the role of local and regional authorities?

In this section we discuss situations where motor industry companies plan to remain active within a region or locality. In the next section (4) we discuss situations in which the motor industry is abandoning an area or is drastically reducing the level of its activities. In reality, the two types of situation are connected. This happens when company decisions to remain in an area are linked to significant restructuring including large-scale loss of employment and significant changes for small and medium enterprises precisely the scenario envisaged by the recent Boston Consulting Group report.

The primary interest of local and regional authorities is to represent communities and local citizens. This does not necessarily mean that they should compete with each other in the traditional sense, to attract investments or government aid. Local and regional authorities can join together to act in their common interests, as the long-standing activities of MILAN reveal.

As well as supporting and representing local citizens and communities, local and regional authorities play an active and positive role in the healthy functioning of the European economy, including the motor industry, just like large companies, small and medium enterprises, trade unions, and national governments. However, that role is not recognized sufficiently, and is not always taken into account in European Union policy formulation.

What economically positive roles do local and regional authorities undertake? What is the best framework for ensuring that their activities are taken into account when policy is formulated at European Union level? In its 1992 policy statement, MILAN proposed three particular areas of European policy in which local and regional authorities already play key economic roles, and in which local and regional authorities can assist in implementation of European-level policy. We can first review this proposal, which is still valid, and then proceed to examine the overall frameworks of partnership through which local and regional authority activities should be included in policy making.

Three examples of local policy which is economically positive and in which local and regional authority activities can aid European-level policy:

(i) Research and Development:

    The Commission has previously recommended that increased resources are devoted to better targeted "research and technical development". However the big vehicle producers are so competitive with each other that they admit themselves very reluctant to co-operate (a requirement for European Union spending on R&D is that it be "pre-competitive", i.e. not benefit any particular firm), even on basic technologies (e.g. batteries for electric cars).

    One solution to this impasse springs from the following observations:

    -   the Commission rightly emphasises the crucial role of components makers to the European motor industry;

- many components makers are currently being called upon by their customers to completely overhaul their organization and research and development functions;

- this can be particularly onerous for small and medium enterprises that cannot devote sufficient specialist resources;

- technical development is defined by the Commission to include new production methods, technically and organisationally, and not just product development.

Therefore a key role for local and regional authorities in diffusing the ability to innovate to the SMEs in the motor components sector can be identified; offering collectively and locally, at grass-roots level, the services that many SMEs need so badly but cannot because of their small size undertake themselves. Many local and regional authorities in Europe, including several members of MILAN, currently have programs designed precisely for this purpose. These existing programs could be improved if developed in combination with European authorities. Other local and regional authorities could learn from the experiences of those that are most active in this regard, through the European networks of local and regional authorities such as those being encouraged by DG XVI, and to which MILAN belongs (e.g. CAR).

(ii) Retraining:

Several commentators have stated recently that it is all very well for the European Union to devote resources to retraining workers displaced by productivity improvements, but this is fruitless if there are no jobs for them to go to. Innovative retraining programmes are needed that "catch" people before they become long-term unemployed, and that are linked to business development needs in their local labour markets. Recent Commission communications make reference to helping the companies with training and retraining needs, but MILAN's view is that retraining should primarily help the displaced employees. Retraining programmes can only be seriously be implemented if they are designed at local level to take into account local needs and local labour markets. It is local and regional authorities and local education institutions that have the necessary experience in this domain, and which can design "holistic" programmes linked to local economic development programmes that do not simply dump retrained workers outside the factory gates.

Here policy-making at European Union level needs to look beyond its current narrow focus on the Social Fund to integrate the kinds of economic development activities currently associated with Regional Fund, which receives no mention at all in recent communications.

We return to the question of how to deal with the human, economic, and physical resources no longer required by the motor industry in section 4, below.

(iii) Social Dialogue:

The need for social dialogue at the regional and local level is emphasized by both the Commission and by the European car producers association ACEA. Indeed ACEA appears to see a specific role for local and regional authorities in this domain. This is to be welcomed, for the definition of social partner and social dialogue should be widened to incorporate all social partners and all types of social dialogue, including but also going beyond the traditional employer-trade union discussions, and especially including the elected representatives of local citizens who depend directly and indirectly upon the motor industry.

However, local-level dialogue does not preclude effective functioning of a Forum on the European Automobile Industry such as the one being held on March 1st 1994. Indeed local-level dialogue will benefit strongly from a European-level Forum, with a "signal" coming from the European level as a stimulus that will legitimate local and regional level discussions. MILAN therefore particularly welcomes the establishment of the Forum.

Local and regional authorities themselves have the legitimacy and the understanding in their regions to call for and to organise local and regional level social dialogue. Indeed the importance of local and regional level dialogue that goes beyond the factory walls cannot be overstated. As discussed in section 2 above ("Local roots of a global industry"), the motor industry in Europe has its foundations in the interactions between companies and local communities. Moreover, the motor industry in each region of Europe is organized somewhat differently from the others, with different histories and different traditions. Significant and rational reorganization of industry must take these facts into account if it is to succeed.

Towards an era of partnership that includes all stakeholders

What should be the institutional framework for discussing the above ideas further? We can take our lead from the new models of industrial organization that are currently being adopted throughout the European motor industry. These models emphasise partnership and the involvement of all stakeholders in determining and carrying out policy decisions.

Many local and regional authorities in Europe have a high level of experience with, and commitment to, operating in partnership with other stakeholders in the local area. It may, however, be the case that larger companies, and some larger institutions such as those operating at European level, have less experience and less commitment in this domain. MILAN would wish to encourage new thinking in this area.

In the end, what may be required i s full recognition of local and regional authorities as social partners. However, this new model is only now emerging, and the institutions that are needed to support it still have to be created. What MILAN believes is necessary, then, is to start to define much more clearly and rationally the role of European Union institutions in this new model, in relation to local and regional authorities.

Policy to rechannel resources no longer needed by the European motor industry

Local and regional economies face a number of problems due to the restructuring of the motor industry in cases where there is significant decline in the level of activity, or where restructuring of operations means that significantly fewer local human, economic and physical resources are required by motor industry companies. These problems can be minimized by effective policies.

The costs of decline

Among the problems that result are:

- direct job loss leading to unemployment, both at assembly companies and their many suppliers,

- job loss and unemployment in support and service industries,

- the threatened disappearance of vital skills bases as the "critical mass" of training infrastructures (at large firms especially) needed to support them is lost,

- break-up of local networks of small and medium firms, threatening the "critical mass" necessary for small and medium enterprises to work together efficiently,

- derelict industrial properties and other unused infrastructures,

- run-down of the high-technology industrial base from which a recovery of technical expertise may not be possible.

The case for European Union action

The European Union has an important role to play in promoting industrial restructuring. However, a balanced policy is needed, one that both incorporates policy and programs instigated at regional and local level (see section 3), and takes regional and local impacts into account. In particular, policy must therefore address the need for rapid re-integration into the local community and local economy of human, economic and physical resources no longer needed by motor industry companies. Moreover, programs must provide the means for this to take place at the local level before these valuable resources are discarded or wasted. This is important for both social and economic reasons.

Indeed a strong case can be made for European Union responsibility for helping to resolve the problems described above. Many problems are by-product results of European Union policies (such as the accelerated restructuring of industry which is precisely one goal of the Single European Market).

MILAN believes that the goal of economic and social cohesion should apply not only at the level of the Union's member states but also at the local scale, where the development of pockets of economic decline and unemployment can have serious consequences for citizens trapped in their own local labour markets, even in regions not on average among the poorest in Europe.

The need for timely intervention

It is well known that restructuring in Europe's motor industry is certain to cause significant problems for motor industry regions and localities. There is no need to wait until after decline has been occurring for several years before taking action.

Furthermore, it is also in the interest of economic efficiency for the European Union as a whole - not just the motor industry sector - to prevent the long-term decline of the local communities that make up the manufacturing base of Europe. Experience reveals that the onset of long-term local economic decline:

-   becomes very difficult to reverse

-   wastes existing local resources (local technical skills bases, local small and medium enterprise networks)

-   requires that extra resources be used over long periods to compensate for lost incomes (income support, social services)

-   effectively puts a whole local manufacturing infrastructure out of action.

It is vital to ensure the renewed viability and prosperity of those motor industry regions and localities which stand to be adversely affected by current industrial restructuring, in order to prevent the onset of precisely the long-term economic decline that in recent decades has affected local communities that were the foundations and roots for industries such as coal, steel and shipbuilding.

Implementation of well planned, efficient, accurately targeted, and above all timely European Union policy instruments could stimulate rapid and viable local economic and community turnaround. In the experience of local authorities with a concert for industrial and regional affairs, it is unfortunate that there remains a wide gap between the activities of DG III and DG XVI of the European Commission. This reflects an outmoded model of policy making where industrial policy and regional policy are viewed as quite separate.

It is in fact possible to adopt a more rational model. Thus MILAN fully supports several of the newer programs that have been adopted and are being considered by the European Union. The European Parliament is to be commended for its initiatives PERIFRA and KONVER, which establish a new model for strategic and active regional policy, which does not wait for local and regional economies to disintegrate before action is taken. If initiatives based on this model received increased resources now, then far fewer resources would be required in future years to attempt the more difficult task of re-developing regions that were already depressed.

Similarly, the principles behind the new definition of Objective 4 regions, emphasising pro-active intervention and retraining of workers prior to redundancy, are fully supported by MILAN local authorities.

The way forward

The main conclusion of this MILAN contribution to the Forum on the European Automobile Industry is that policy directed towards the needs of motor industry local economies and local communities should form part of a balanced industrial and regional policy that focuses upon both:

-   increasing the competitiveness of the motor industry directly, and involving local and regional authorities in the planning and implementation of policies; and,

-   re-channelling those human, economic and physical resources that the industry no longer needs, in the interests both of social cohesion at the local scale and of improvement of the efficiency of the European economy as a whole.

What is essential is to move forward on both these fronts is to ensure that the skills and experience of local and regional authorities are incorporated into the policy-making process and into the program implementation process.

MILAN speaks for local and regional authorities across the European Union in giving the assurance that those local and regional authorities are willing and able to play their part in the future successful development of the motor industry in Europe and of the communities that support the industry.

Mr Mihr:

Thank you very much Mr Firth.

We have three questions which have been submitted.

Mr Beger, Executive Secretary of the ACEA, would like to ask Dr Camerana why he did not invest in Germany. Dr Camerana?

Dr Camerana:

We didn't have the opportunity to invest in Germany. In 1986 when we started this rationalisation programme, we bought a number of companies in France, in England, in Spain and in Italy, but we didn't have the opportunity to buy a company in Germany. This is the main reason why. I suspect that it would be rather difficult to buy a German company, at that time. Maybe today it would be easier.

Mr Mihr:

Thank you very much. Now we have another question, this for Mr Adelt, again from Dr Beger. What about structural plans in VW? Not just conjunctural, short-term changes, but improvements in competitiveness. Ms Ernst de la Graete also asked a question. Would you care to answer this too, please.

📖 *Mr Adelt:*

Well, it is very easy to answer the question about the rumour of VW moving from Forest in Brussels to Asia. This is crazy. I simply fail to see how such rumours get going in the first place. No.

As to structural models, in the first place of course, they help to solve our structural problems. Our cost structures are improving. You will probably know that this now covers the whole of our fixed cost wage bill, which since it is decreasing, will lower the break-even point. In addition, we have managed to achieve the flexibility necessary to start a process of continuous improvement, and this is a very decisive element of this.

Mr Mihr:

Well, I think we have reached the end of this broad-ranging workshop. I should like to thank everyone on the platform, and everyone in the room. I hope that there will be a follow-up to this important event, but we do hope that there will be an attempt to hold discussions in a similar fashion at the places the industry is located, to consider the Europe of the regions, to lower the risk for some regions through pooling our efforts.

Thank you very much, ladies and gentlemen.

WORKSHOP 3

SUMMARY REPORT

MR K.H. MIHR
MEMBER OF THE
EUROPEAN PARLIAMENT

Prof. Morgan

Prof. Morgan referred to the fact that the automobile industry was undergoing the biggest process of restructuring since the war. Apart from problems of industrial adjustment, this process was also creating problems of social and economic renewal at regional level. He concluded that the future prospects for the survival of the European automobile industry depended to a crucial extent on the relationship between manufacturers and suppliers.

The traditional car centres in Europe were not capable of surviving in their present form, and the car industry would as far as possible therefore have to copy the Japanese model as regards the reduction of costs, working methods and manufacturer-supplier relationships.

Germany in particular had fallen considerably behind its competitors in recent years in terms of cost structure, turnover and sales price, with the result that German companies would be constructing new factories outside the Federal Republic and at the same time reducing production in the old ones.

Prof. Morgan proposed two approaches:

(1) Improving cost effectiveness by means of a more intensive supplier-producer relationship (vertical improvement);

(2) Improving cost effectiveness by means of more innovative R&D policy among suppliers themselves (horizontal improvement).

At European level, a solution should be found for the automobile industry similar to the KONVER Programme. The horizontal measures planned by the Commission could be supported by means of such a programme. In addition DGs III, XII, XVI and XXIII of the Commission should co-operate more closely.

Mr Dufeil

Mr Dufeil spoke about the Union's Structural Funds, emphasising the fact that these Funds played a key role in any structural change. They were intended to create the necessary conditions for the competitiveness of industry and at the same time to help to avoid job losses. The Structural Funds (1994-1999) therefore also include the special task of the development of human capital. He went on to describe the measures within the Structural Funds which were of particular interest to the automobile industry:

- vocational training needed to be brought into line with structural change;

- the second measure concerned the ADAPT initiative, co-operation measures within the Community. The aim of this initiative was also to promote co-operation and partnerships between research centres, training establishments, suppliers and producers;

- the Community initiative for the promotion of SMEs was also important for the car industry and in particular for suppliers;

- the traditional form of the Structural Funds, namely conventional aid for investment and infrastructure, was of major importance to the automobile industry.

Mr Adelt

The structural crisis in the automobile industry was not yet over. For Volkswagen, this meant that productivity had to improved in order to catch up with the Japanese and US car industries.

If only conventional measures were taken, the crisis would mean a loss for Volkswagen of about 30 000 jobs in and around Lower Saxony alone, an area which was almost completely dependent on this industry.

New ways of reducing costs and saving as many jobs as possible had to be found. Productivity also had to be increased.

Measures such as early retirement, the reorganization of labour and a four-day week would help to reduce unit costs, to increase productivity and therefore to improve competitiveness without the need to shed any jobs. The company would remain free and could be flexible to adjust production upwards or downwards according to demand.

Volkswagen had also introduced a flexible system of working which enabled its staff to stop work for 4 to 6 months if they so wished.

Volkswagen could serve as an example to other companies in the car industry.

Mr Maragall

In Spain, there was a network linking the cities in which the automobile industry was located: RECA.

The increasing problems in the car industry and the resulting job losses were forcing the cities to find new solutions. The service sector, for example, provided opportunities for people with low qualifications to find a new job. More new jobs could also be created in the tourist industry, for example. However, it was expected that only 25 to 35% of car workers who lost their jobs would be able to find alternative employment in this way. What was needed was therefore an alternative industrial policy which helped people to become reintegrated into the working world.

Investment policy had to go hand in hand with technological progress. Most of the difficulties were in areas in which the car industry was successful because of the low personnel costs. Research and training had to be improved and politicians would have to work closely together with private business. The city of Barcelona was co-operating with VW-Seat on the factory in the Zona Franca. The city owned the building land and had a joint share in the factory together with the region. The city would do everything it possibly could to bring the crisis to an end.

One example of this was the Euroconference which would take place in Barcelona in June on the subject of cars, cables and recycling. This conference would bring together industrial managers and representatives of the municipal authorities so that a way out of the crisis could be sought on a common basis.

The Panel

The panel members briefly introduced themselves and went on to discuss the regional problems facing the automobile industry.

Dr Camerana discussed the problems of the supply industry and noted that this branch of industry only had any prospects if it moved with the automobile industry in terms of location and formed alliances.

Mrs Ernst de la Graete explained the environmental problems facing the automobile industry: CO_2 emissions, recycling, the necessary support for public transport and social problems.

Mr Firth, the representative of the MILAN network, described the network and how it worked.

FORUM ON THE EUROPEAN AUTOMOBILE INDUSTRY

BRUSSELS - PALAIS DES CONGRÈS - 1 MARCH 1994

WORKSHOP 4

ENHANCING CO-OPERATION IN THE AUTOMOBILE INDUSTRY
- AN AGENDA FOR ACTION -

Moderator:	Ms Carole Tongue, MEP	European Parliament Rapporteur on the European Car Industry
New Partnership Strategies in the Car Industry	Mr D. Bower	Personnel Director of Rover Group
	Mr J. Adams	Deputy Secretary General of the British Transport and General Workers Union
New Partnership Strategies in the Components Industry	Mr K. Ellegast	Director of Phoenix AG
Panel:	Mr G. Crauser	Director for Consumer Goods Industries, European Commission
	Mr A. Sainjon	Member of the European Parliament
	Mr F. Haberl	Vice-President of CECRA, the European Committee for Motor Trades and Repairs
	Dr D. Gregory	Trade Union Research Unit, Ruskin College, Oxford

📖 *Ms Tongue:*

Please take your seats as soon as possible - we're under heavy time pressure. We're going to be able to go on a little longer, and we thank our interpreters for this, but we still have to respect their time and energy. So let us begin.

My name in Carole Tongue. I'm a Member of the European Parliament. I represent an area in the United Kingdom which is called London East, in which is situated the Ford plant at Dagenham - hence my own personal interest in the industry - and I'm very happy that there are people from both the management and the Trade Unions from Dagenham here today.

If I could just briefly say who we have here on this last Workshop: we have Mr David Bower, who is the Personnel Director of the Rover Group; Mr Jack Adams, who is the Deputy Secretary General of the Transport and General Workers Union; we have Mr Konrad Ellegast, who is Managing Director of Phoenix Components in Germany, Mr Guy Crauser, who is Director for the Consumer Goods Industries at the European Commission; Mr André Sainjon, who is a Member of the European Parliament, and is a good colleague of mine, and also specialises in the industry; Mr Fritz Haberl, Vice President of CECRA, the distributors' federation; and finally Dr Dennis Gregory, who is from the Trade Union Research Unit at Ruskin College, Oxford.

We're here in this last Workshop to look at enhancing co-operation and partnership in the automobile industry, and hopefully coming forward with some very practical ideas - an agenda for action - for going forward from this Forum today.

The first person I would like to ask to speak is Mr David Bower, but before he goes to the podium, I would just like to throw out a few ideas on the issues we would like to discuss in this Workshop:

- better relations and partnership inside the industry;

- the issue of European Works councils has been raised;

- the issue of training within the industry;

- the partnership between suppliers and manufacturers, which has to be improved in the interests of greater competitivity;

- partnership - and whilst this was raised in the last Workshop, we can take it up again here - between actors at a regional level, to improve the securing of the funds that the European Commission is putting forward under Objective 4 and under the ADAPT Initiative;

- finally, and very importantly, indeed one of the main reasons we're here today, the partnership between all of us, all the players concerned in the industry, and the European Commission.

First of all, Mr David Bower, Personnel Director of Rover Group. Thank you Mr Bower.

📖 ___Mr Bower:___

Good afternoon.

Firstly, let me apologise on behalf of John Towers, who for personal reasons isn't able to be with us this afternoon, but I am personally delighted to be here.

New Partnership Strategies in the Car Industry

My purpose today is not to comment on the new partnership which has made Rover a little more famous during the past four weeks, but on another partnership which we have, more quietly, forged over the past four years with our workforce, and to which I will return in a moment.

New partnership strategies within the car industry are not simply desirable, they are an essential element in the strategic imperative of the industry.

These partnerships must embrace all activities - from suppliers and vehicle assemblers through distribution channels - on an extended enterprise basis.

This idea is nothing new, and many European car makers are developing such partnerships as part of their business strategies.

Where Rover might be an interesting example is that we firmly believe it is possible through partnership arrangements to achieve the competitiveness of greenfield operations by working <u>within</u> accepted traditional conventions and <u>within</u> existing brownfield factories.

Therefore our "New Deal" employee agreement signed nearly two years ago recognises the right of Trade Unions to continue to represent our employees, and the right of our employees to employment within the company or our extended enterprise.

For their part, the Trades Unions have shown a high degree of understanding and a commitment to full workplace flexibility, mobility of labour, multi-skilling and continuous improvement and learning, which has played a significant part in the revival of Rover.

- Rover has been without industrial disputes for 6 years. It pioneered two-year pay agreements in the UK in the early 1980s.

- It has managed, without conflict, the painful transition from an unsuccessful volume producer to an increasingly successful specialist manufacturer.

- Productivity and efficiency have risen from the worst in Europe to among the best.

- Quality standards have risen through employees taking responsibility for the quality of their work instead of a system of "inspecting in" quality at the end of the production process.

Such partnerships are indispensable to the survival of individual companies.

However, within the context of the European motor industry as a whole, there is a need for more broadly based partnerships between vehicle companies themselves and between legislators and the industry to meet the external competitive challenges we face.

In the time allotted to me I will confine my remarks to two areas of outstanding performance where strategic partnerships are fundamental to the future of our industry: - **technology and training**.

Research and Technology Funding partnerships are essential in Europe. We have fragmented and historically-nationally-based motor industries who face off to the more unified structures of support in the US and Japan. No market is more overcrowded, more competitive or more in need of a co-ordinated approach to technology.

Rover is involved in some 40 European research and technology projects, mostly through the Joint Research Council and with European Commission funding.

These are already bearing fruit in areas such as traffic management, intelligent accident avoidance, lightweight vehicles and environmental advances.

However, much more needs to be done, and the Joint Research Council itself is in the process of changing to EUCAR - the European Council for Automotive Research and Development.

A further major step forward has been the "Advanced Information Technology" Programme involving auto and aerospace manufacturers. This brings a new approach and perspective to research and technology which we warmly welcome.

Under this far-reaching programme, the parameters are being set by user industries themselves during an 18-month initial stage followed by a five-year delivery programme.

However, the question has to be posed: is Europe doing enough? By comparison, there is a concrete, focused programme in the US with the government diverting space-related research to auto industry application in fuel-efficient vehicles, and in Japan there is MITI-sponsored research in next generation vehicle catalysts.

Both are very formidable programmes, and there is no European equivalent. EUCAR can do so much, but funding is still not remotely on the scale available, for example, to USCAR, its American equivalent.

Training Partnerships. When it comes to training partnerships, the answer to the same question, "Is Europe doing enough?" - has to be, in my view, an emphatic "No".

Those partnerships which do exist are fragmented between various EC Directorates with little co-ordination, and are considerably over-subscribed and under-funded.

If we truly believe that people should be given the chance of continuous learning to improve themselves and their workplace, we simply cannot let the vital issue of training fall mainly upon individual companies.

Rover is not a large company, but it spends £35 million each year out of its own pocket on training for its 33,000 employees - which makes it the largest provider of learning in the UK outside the educational sector.

As part of our progress towards achieving world-class performance levels we have measured and benchmarked all activities which contribute to our business.

They divide into "Hard" and "Soft" issues.

The hard issues are those which we can fully, or almost fully control, such as efficiency, quality, right-first-time, cost reduction and so forth.

These are challenging but relatively straightforward activities.

It is the soft issues - like the appropriateness of education to industry, lifetime learning and training initiatives which are of prime importance to our people strategies, and with which we would wish to have greater involvement.

The current approach in partnerships is piecemeal - joint activity with a UK training enterprise council here, and with a university there, and with national governments often having varying interpretations of what constitutes legitimate publicly-funded training.

As in a number of areas, the training ground across Europe is by no means level or equitable.

The car industry is at the forefront of technological innovation. We have long realised that it is not technology itself or automation which produces results. It is highly trained, highly motivated people within a committed workforce who create wealth, employment and competitive advantage.

This cannot be successfully achieved without a framework of training. Structural change and technology will inevitably bring about reductions in employment in some areas, while creating opportunities in others.

Without flexibility, without means and methods of continuous learning, people will not be able to adapt to changing circumstances or be in a position to take advantage of new avenues of work.

In Rover's case the framework of co-operation within its own control and resources is in place and working fairly successfully.

What is required at both national and European levels is a more structured framework of objectives and programmes similar to, and compatible with, the research and technology framework.

We need to encourage re-skilling, multi-skilling and learning within the extended enterprise culture. Such a foundation would allow employers to develop more strategic partnerships and longer-term relationships. Rover Group's benefits from participation in joint Research and Technology Programmes far exceed the usual 50 per cent funding level: in 1993, we estimate up to ten times our investment. The Community must work to achieve similar levels of benefits from its Social Fund programmes.

Thank you very much for your attention.

Ms Tongue:

Thank you very much for your brevity and clarity. Can I now invite Mr Jack Adams, Deputy Secretary General of the Transport and General Workers Union.

Mr Adams:

Colleagues,

I am pleased to be making this contribution because, as many of you will know, the Transport and General Workers' Union represents in excess of 100,000 car and car components workers in the UK and Éire, and has a vested interest in developing positive relations between workers and employers in the face of new competitive and production challenges.

I believe there are three crucial dimensions to the question of new partnership strategies.

In the first place, we need to address the relationship that exists, or could exist, between worker and employee at the point of production and at company level.

Secondly, I believe that we need to consider relationships at a corporate and institutional level, and by that I mean that relations between multinational companies and the organisations or bodies that represent their workforces.

Finally, I do believe that we face a responsibility to develop a co-operative approach with European policy makers to match our activities on the domestic scene.

These, then, are the crucial ingredients that we need to look at in developing a partnership in this industry.

I start by saying that unless we work together, we are bound to fail.

Quite aside from the flexible production and Human Resource Management debates, we are faced with a classic overproduction crisis which will prove a competitive weakness in the global marketplace.

Add to that the discouraging news from the Boston report on components, which estimates that between 400,000 and half a million job losses will be required for European companies to reach global levels of efficiency.

I think these problems are now beginning to be recognised. We have welcomed the two Tongue reports on the industry, and we have followed closely the progress on the Bangemann Communication on the future of the automotive industry. We are also aware of the interesting work being done by ACEA in response to these reports.

There is no point in talking around issues at an important event such as this - we need to understand each other fully - let me be clear that, as far as we are concerned, the scale of the problems faced, the potential human dislocation involved, and the political will needed to effect some change, are such that a resolution cannot be found that does not involve the workers affected and the trade unions that represent them.

The value of the people within the industry must be recognised.

Partnership strategies are not some vague philosophical or moral notion to which we may personally be attached to a greater or lesser extent; they are an essential condition for us to get this industry established with a global future.

What then are our approaches to partnership at the three levels I have referred to?

Firstly, we believe firmly that participation and partnership need to start as closely as possible to the point of production, and that means real and meaningful dialogue, not just communication and information. If we don't get our productive processes right, and motivate, support and empower our workforces, all else will fail.

That also means that we need to recognise, rather than challenge, the legitimate role of trade unions in the workplace.

I think that those of you who are familiar with our landmark agreement with Rover will recognise that it is possible to introduce radical change to allay the natural fears of workers, and to do so in a way that is beneficial to all parties concerned. We are satisfied by that agreement, and would point to it as an example of the way in which lean production methods and new personnel philosophies can be introduced consensually and with the full co-operation of the workers' representatives on established brown field sites.

The second point I would like to make on relations at the plant or production levels is that if you combine the objectives of HRM and lean production with the very real problem of global and European overcapacity, the conclusion that few automotive employees would escape from is that new working methods are required in order for them to work themselves out of a job.

Clearly, such perceptions are hardly a recipe for co-operation and consensus over the introduction of production changes.

That is why we believe that flexibility commitments from workers need to be matched by job and wage security guarantees from employers. I would again point to the Rover agreement as one which embodies that approach, and which has given all sides the confidence to change and to adapt to new circumstances.

On the second dimension, that is relations at a corporate level, I have to say that I find myself somewhat surprised at the gap between the rhetoric of partnership espoused by many major companies, and their evident distaste for the modest proposal contained in the European Works Council Directive.

Partnership to work has to be informed partnership.

Increasingly, our companies and industries are facing problems of a transnational nature; employees need to be mobilised to meet new challenges, political forces need to be tapped to effect change, Europe-wide strategies need to be developed.

We believe that European Works Councils could play a key role in information exchange, and in developing common positions or principles where our interests coincide.

The third area that needs our consideration is partnership and co-operation at European Union level. Increasingly, policies that affect our sector are made at this level, and co-operation, dialogue and debate of the sort that we are having today are crucial if we are to speak with one voice on behalf of the industry and the livelihoods that it sustains.

If we look at the environmental considerations; at the question of trade relations such as the debate on the Japan-EC car accord that Bangemann has opened up; if we consider the question of funding under the new Objective 4 Training Fund; on all of these issues we need to keep open regular lines of communication and dialogue.

I know that the European Metalworkers' Federation has played an important role, as have the affiliated unions such as ourselves, in seeking to articulate our concerns to the Commission and European Union Member States' national governments.

We, within the T&G, have worked particularly closely with our colleagues in the European Parliament to stimulate and support positive policies for car makers and car workers. The industry has also mobilised its forces effectively to articulate manufacturers' and employers' concerns.

But I believe that we need to go further. We are all stakeholders in this industry, and the challenges that face us mean, as I said earlier, that we can only be effective if we work together, and quite frankly we cannot afford to fail.

I believe that we should make a clear recommendation to the Commission and the European Parliament arising from today's conference that they give serious consideration to the establishment of a standing Technical or Social Forum on the European Automobile Industry, and only that way do we think that the real challenges, the partnership means, can be addressed.

Thank you very much.

Ms Tongue:

Thank you very much. Now Mr Ellegast of Phoenix Components, Germany.

Mr Ellegast:

Ladies and Gentlemen, I am please that medium-sized industry has a chance to speak today - and not just the very large companies which are known worldwide.

Phoenix has a turnover of DM 1 Billion, 700 employees, several plants in Germany, but also a number in France, Spain, Italy and Turkey.

Growing need for co-operation in the automobile industry - necessary measures

The entire European automobile industry, manufacturers and suppliers, is currently in the throes of a dramatic slump. Production fell by over 20% in some cases in 1993, with the United Kingdom proving the only exception. The coming year offers little prospect of recovery.

The fall in volume led to an escalation of the already bitter price war, with the result that very few suppliers can have shown a profit in 1993. There was a steady rise in the number of bankruptcies, a trend that is set to continue in 1994.

The crisis for German suppliers was compounded by the considerable fluctuations in exchange rates in the European system between the Deutschmark, the peseta, the pound and the lira. Devaluations of 20% and more have given foreign competitors the edge under the global sourcing system, which is used intensively by all European car manufacturers.

The crisis also brought glaringly to light the fact that the supply industry, like the car manufacturers themselves, is undergoing a structural crisis. The important study carried out by the Massachusetts Institute of Technology in 1990 (The second revolution in the car industry) pinpointed three problem areas: higher costs, poorer time management and a quality shortfall compared with Japanese products.

One major reason why costs are higher in Europe is the huge variety of parts here compared with Japan. To give just one example from our own company: we have over 3 600 different types of manifold, where a comparable firm in Japan producing, moreover, twice the volume, gets by with just 300. Any supplier could provide a whole range of similar examples. At a guess, I would say that the variety of parts available is at least ten times as great as in Japan.

The problems for suppliers therefore run very deep, and solving them requires a three-pronged approach consisting of:

1. Radical restructuring by firms.

2. Problem-solving in partnership with customers and suppliers.

3. Improvement of the political framework.

<u>Point 1</u>: **Radical restructuring by firms**

A large number of suppliers have begun work in time on optimizing production and administration to achieve "lean company" conditions. This means preventing any kind of wastage, e.g. in terms of storage times, transport routes or unnecessary administration.

The "lean company" project centres around the involvement of the workforce. Employees must be trained to carry out a number of tasks as part of a group or, for instance, to perform simple maintenance tasks themselves. They must be motivated to work out suggestions for improving their job. This requires intensive training in analysing and solving problems. The intellectual potential of the workforce has not been sufficiently exploited in the past, and radical changes are needed. Hierarchical structures must be increasingly dismantled and more responsibility delegated to employees. They in turn must learn to think and act in entrepreneurial fashion. The Japanese have shown that it can be done.

This approach has been applied in our company for the last two years. To give you some idea of what it entails, here is a diagram showing the main building blocks of the project. The results so far have been very encouraging. The "lean company" project carried out over the last two years in accordance with a strict timetable is now giving way to an on-going improvement process. No supplier will be spared this radical overhaul if it wants to maintain its place in the market. This applies in particular to German suppliers, who will only survive if they can compete successfully in the international arena. There is growing competition from cheaper locations such as Eastern Europe, where wage costs are about a twentieth of those in Germany.

However, it is important for us as suppliers that the car manufacturers should not use price as the sole criterion in competition, but should also compare capacity for development, reliability of supply and structural financial stability .

<u>Point 2</u>: **Problem-solving in partnership with customers and suppliers**

In addition to these very difficult structural changes within each company, there are certain areas which can only be tackled in partnership with the manufacturers and suppliers. Through projects of this kind we can work together to effect improvements in the three main areas where we are lagging behind Japanese firms, namely quality, time management and costs. A number of car manufacturers are involved in co-operative projects of this kind. Examples include Mercedes-Benz's "Tandem" project and Fiat's "Co-makership" scheme. Under these schemes the supplier has to be involved in development at a much earlier stage in order to avoid duplication. For example, the task of reducing the range of parts, which I referred to earlier, can only be carried out in conjunction with the manufacturers.

We have carried out similar projects with our own suppliers which have also produced good results. Furthermore, I feel that more thought should be given to the scope for co-operation between competitors in the supply industry. Each company must be aware of its strengths and weaknesses as regards different product lines. Where the weaker product lines are concerned, they must consider to what extent these might be improved by out sourcing or concentration with other firms. Another aspect of this is co-operation with firms in other countries. It no longer makes sense for each firm to set up investment capacity abroad, which is rarely fully utilised. Closer co-operation is essential here if we are to avoid massive squandering of capital.

Point 3:   **Improvement of the political framework**

The third strategic area which must be tackled by both car manufacturers and suppliers is the broad spectrum of the public sector. I believe that it is useless for industry to trim down unless the public sector shows signs of becoming more efficient and cost-effective.

The costs incurred by firms in terms of charges, taxes, approval procedures, compliance with environmental legislation, etc. have seen a sharp increase in recent years, while prices in the supply industry have been falling. Costs imposed by the public sector, and this of course includes Brussels, must be reduced. Lean company projects must be conducted in the public sector too, and outdated structures in subsidies policy must be abolished. We can no longer afford to prop up old industrial sectors and agriculture for years with sums running into billions. This kind of squandering also has got to stop. Unless changes are made, the European car industry, despite its best efforts, will have little chance in long-term international competition.

Thank you for your attention.

Ms Tongue:

Thank you, Mr Ellegast, again for such clarity and brevity. I should like to move on to the Panel now, to some of the questions which have already been raised by friends here today.

When I hand over to Mr Crauser, a Director in the Commission, I should like to ask him to address, in addition to what he was going to say, some of the questions raised both by our speakers but also from the floor of the Forum.

There has been a very clear demand that the Commission have a very clear programme for the car industry. This has not just been mentioned in this Workshop, but in previous ones too. Mr Beger from ACEA would like to ask Mr Crauser to address what he believes to be the present deficiencies of the existing training programmes that will be supported by the European Commission, and Dr H. Soboll, Vice President of Information Technology at Daimler-Benz, asks the Commission about the possibility of greater collaborative horizontal research projects to be supported by the European Commission.

Finally, a key point which was made, a very practical and logistical point which I know a lot of people here feel very strongly about, is that if one is to have a very clear programme for the industry, then you have to have very clear co-ordination within the European Commission itself, which we know has to work across a number of different Directorates General. Perhaps you'd like to comment, Mr Crauser, as to how it can be better co-ordinated - for example over the different DGs who are concerned with the industry.

📖 *Mr Crauser:*

Thank you Ms Tongue.

I should simply like to point out, like several speakers have before me, how important we feel that this increased co-operation and these new relationships based on partnerships are.

For us, it is really in these co-operative relationships that the Community can make a contribution to added value. The new co-operative relationships and partnerships are, in total, the opposite of what one might call *le soupoudrage*, that's to say spreading efforts all over the place, without any great efficiency. Our policy, as you may have realised from reading our recent document - which was distributed this morning[1] - is effectively to unite everybody's efforts. This is the case in every area.

We were speaking earlier about research and development. It is quite clear that the funds that the Community or the Member States can put at the disposition of the automobile industry in the sphere of research and development can only be effective when they are concentrated on projects which have been set up by the industry itself. That is to say projects which have been set up not by civil servants, but by industrialists, in order that they should have an effect in as horizontal a fashion as possible, and be available to everyone. This is the opposite of a "Pick a Winner" policy.

Also, we should encourage the industrialists to reach consensus, and to continue to reinforce, and to build upon, the level of co-operation that they have already implemented to develop research and development projects which can be applied in the different areas, which will be those of the Commission's Fourth Framework Programme, research and development.

Ms Tongue, on this subject, you asked why co-ordination could not be improved among the European Institutions. In fact, when you draw up industrial policy in a horizontal fashion, that's to say you develop themes and actions which are available to all, it is absolutely necessary that these instruments, being horizontal, be co-ordinated among themselves.

We believe that we have succeeded, in principle in any case: in producing this Communication, you will have noted that in this programme we have brought together Internal Market considerations, those of research and development, the new ideas about Structural Funds, the problems of commercial policy, all themes which are covered by different departments within the Commission. It is clear that many things remain to be done. For example, to improve the level of co-ordination in implementing the research and development programmes, we decided - and this at Commission level, it was not DG III which took this decision, we decided this together - we decided on an informational structure, which would allow research and development initiatives within the

---

[1]   The Communication from Commission to the Council and the European Parliament on the European Automobile Industry, COM(94)49 final (see annex).

framework of the Fourth Programme to be appreciated by the Commission, the Director-ates General for Industry, Research and Development etc. It will obviously be very important to arrive at a situation where such projects are not broken up into small pieces, but are viewed by the Commission services in their entirety, and following the same logic as that by which they were drawn up.

I gave the example of research and development; the same thing is valid for the Structural Funds. I am not sure that there is a great deal of contradiction between what we are doing at present in terms of training and what will be the new generation of training. We must take account of the fact that this new generation will have some new characteristics not necessarily compatible with those of the old generation. This is about complying with the needs that the changes in industry as we know them. That's to say to try to converge towards what we have just heard, i.e. training in the new production methods, training to bring SMEs towards partnerships with larger companies, training for this new type of co-operation between, for example, the assemblers and the compo-nents producers, etc.

The same issues of co-operation and partnership are also the basis of our work as regards the Internal Market. When we encouraged the launch of the Auto-Oil programme, a project involving the automobile manufacturing industry and the petro-leum industry to try to set up a new programme for the next stage in the reduction of motor vehicle emissions levels, it a was a new form of co-operation par excellence which we put forward.

When we talk about selective distribution, what exactly are we talking about? The fundamental justification for selective distribution is the narrow relationship of partner-ship which must exist between the motor vehicle manufacturers and the distribution network and all the different services that this implies. So here too we have co-opera-tion at the centre of the debate.

This is also valid for external commercial policy. Just a moment ago someone alluded to what the Americans are doing as regards their components industry, and the competition it is facing from the Japanese. This is only the tip of the iceberg, this is clear, this is political pressure, but one needs to bear in mind that under this political pressure there is the long history of preparation for co-operation between the American companies and their Japanese counterparts to make possible the participation of the component manufacturers in the manufacture of the systems which will constitute the new Japanese models. There are "Design-In" seminars, which were defined a long time ago, in which the component manufacturers try to get involved at the conception stage of the design of these new models in order to become eligible for exporting their prod-ucts not only to Japan, but also to the other Asian markets which are heavily influenced by Japanese technology.

Clearly the Commission's policy is that this co-operation should emerge, and that value-added should be achieved by these companies. Clearly it should be recognised that the co-operative relationships between the different operators is essentially, if not exclusively, down to the industry itself. It is down to the industry itself to examine this new technology, these new working methods, to design their own training programmes, and to find the best formulae with their social partners for their own cases. We heard about a very relevant example from the representative from Volkswagen earlier this afternoon.

So, I do not know if I have replied to all your questions. I replied on the issue of co-ordination amongst the services of the Commission. This is getting better, but it can be improved further. Is there some contradiction between what we are doing now and what we are going to do on the issue of training? Well, not really a contradiction, but there is a new generation of training programmes, which are necessary in the context of the industrial changes we are confronted with at the moment. What can be done as regards the collaboration between industries in terms of research and development? Well, I think I answered that question too: it is absolutely fundamental that the industry itself gets together to conceive of the most important projects, which should be financed or co-financed either by the Community or by the Member States, or not at all if this is their wish, as expressed by the last speaker.

Thank you.

Ms Tongue:

Thank you very much Mr Crauser. I won't make any comment - I'll allow others to comment on what you have been saying. I'm sure they will.

Mr Malcolm Harbour, Director of the International Car Distribution Programme, said to me, quite rightly, that I had made no mention at all of the players in the car retail and servicing sector. We are trying to cover, as you know, an awful lot today. In this respect we are happy to have with us today Mr Fritz Haberl, who is the Vice President of CECRA, which is the European Federation of Distributors, and I would like to ask him now to say a few words to us to make an important contribution in a sector that employs at least 2 million people in the Community. Mr Haberl.

Mr Haberl:

Thank you very much Ms Tongue.

Ladies and gentlemen, when we hear the notion of improved partnership in the auto-mobile industry - and somebody did say that this would reinforce our competitiveness - first and foremost one talks about co-operation between management and employees, including Trade Unions, I suppose, or is one thinking about co-operation between manu-facturers, in order to produce components which will suit several different models?

I think probably the strongest partnership exists between the automobile manufactur-ers and their distribution network, and that's where one finds real partnership. Perhaps we are not thinking about this enough.

With respect to block exemptions, I think it is very important to do a bit of thinking about this. It's a question of training the workforce, and that is a costly business because technology is changing all the time. Dealers have to be trained, of course, but we are also talking about technical information - manuals, shopfloor electronics, etc., and there's even talk now of satellite broadcasting in the workshop. All this is part of partnership - communication is vital where vehicles are purchased and sold.

Here also environmental considerations are vital. One must be sure that when a vehicle is sold, environmental requirements are fulfilled. This continues to apply after the day the vehicle is sold as well. So we have been talking about improving partnerships and enhancing competitiveness. This morning I heard from Mr Murray that the European automobile industry is not competitive, firstly because it is fragmented, and secondly because it has a network of contracts. Is this not a contradiction? Why should this be bad for competition? Mr Murray was the only consumer representative, unfortunately. I think that AIT, with millions of motorists behind it, and all the automobile clubs around Europe, might have been very welcome here as spokespersons for the consumer. If there is another Forum, I hope they will be invited.

The car is not a high-tech product, but I do think that cars are going to become more and more similar. This means that after-sales service is going to become more and more important. The individual consumer becomes less and less important by this token.

Unlike household items like fridges, the vehicle is constantly on the move, and all dealers throughout Europe are going to be able to maintain the same standard. I think this is basic to the trade, and that special regulation is required here.

You can get spare parts for ten years after your model has ceased to be produced, and this is vital to the network. Daily co-operation with the manufacturer is vital to getting a competitive edge, so that what is necessary can be provided. But is competition just a question of quantity? I feel it is more a question of quality. In Germany, we used to have half as many chemists shops as we have today, but I do not think that this has altered competitiveness. We need lean distribution as well as lean production. I think that there are probably too many dealers in Europe. In the US they sell four times as many cars as we do in Europe with the same number of dealers. So if we need more competition, we might find that our quality is going to diminish, and this is bad for the consumer.

Thank you.

Ms Tongue:

Thank you very much. I should now like to turn to my colleague from the European Parliament, Mr André Sainjon, MEP from France, to make a short contribution, and hopefully to direct comments again to what he sees as the role of the Commission in ensuring the future competitiveness of this industry, particularly where training and Social Dialogue are concerned. André?

📖 *Mr Sainjon:*

Thank you, *Présidente*.

To reply to these questions, I should first like to state my agreement to a certain number of points which have been made today. I consider that the automobile industry is a major economic and social issue in Europe.

Saying this I should like to reflect on the subject of companies. Firms are for me by definition a privileged place for developing social relationships. I believe that this point will not escape anyone here. I would even go as far as to say that no-one here should **let** this point escape them. The success of a firm, a group, an industry, does not depend on technical or commercial success, but depends also on its degree of success in social terms. I believe that a company is not an abstract term; it is a living entity, made up of men and women who give the best of themselves to the success of the company.

In my opinion, a correct industrial strategy cannot be defined today without taking into consideration the social dimension - one might even call it the human dimension - notably when we look at the reality of Europe today, and the significance of unemployment. All our reflections should be directed at finding a solution to this serious problem. If not, Europe will dash the hopes of millions of young people.

It is interesting to examine this problem in the context of the automobile industry. I see this industry as one which has strong traditions in the social context. I believe that these traditions constitute today, regarding the problems with which we are confronted in the case of the restructuring and the globalisation of this business and the increased level of competitiveness, that these traditions are a trump card for resolving the considerable changes with which this industry is confronted. I think that if one wants to move reasonably towards solutions, we have to talk to one another. We have to talk to one another a lot. Lots of dialogue, in order to get everyone to understand these problems, and to go on from this point to define solutions which do not smash either the industry or the level of employment in it - in other words the people. It is another responsibility which we have, as much at the level of company director as at the level of the Trade Unions, the European Parliament or the Commission. It is a major responsibility. I believe that it is absolutely necessary, on the basis of what has been done today, to engage the process of dialogue, and this at every level, since there is a general and collective interest so to do. At least this is my conviction.

At the same time we would thereby allow it to be made clear that we really do want to set up a genuine industrial policy, capable of confronting the great challenges with which we are confronted. This is why I think there should be a follow-up to this conference. One can see that lots of issues have been raised, and that these need further debate.

At the same time, it seems that we have entered into a new phase where group dialogue is turning into research into problems associated notably with employment. I was very interested to hear what the representative from Volkswagen said earlier about new working methods and working hours, and about what has been agreed in close consultation with the Trade Unions in the company. I am not saying that this model is applicable everywhere, but this is one example amongst several which could be taken in part, and which resolves these problems in part. The issue of training was well covered in the explanation he gave us as well.

So, I think these examples merit being taken on board and understood by us all, particularly by the Commission. This is why I would like to see us drawing up, perhaps even today, a rather more concrete approach to these issues of what we call Social Partnership, for every level. First at the level of the industrial groupings in the automobile industry in each country, but also at the level of the European automobile industry, and when I say this I mean the manufacturers and the component suppliers together. I think we have a weakness in this area regarding the component suppliers. Let us be sure not to let this sector escape our attention. It is particularly important in terms of research and development, and I for one am very concerned about it.

Dialogue with the Commission must be developed. I feel that we should be moving towards implementation at the level of technical working groups, including all those who work in the automobile industry, and all those who use automobiles. This appears to me to be crucial, that we should learn to work like this at Commission level. I am tempted to say, talking about the Commission, and not because we are in a pre-election period, that I think the Commission does a lot of very useful work, but it needs to convey the impression of being rather more, well, *human*. I think you will understand what I mean. Closer to the people. It is because I feel this way that I think it is important that the strategic decisions taken by the Commission should be taken in the light of a real concerted effort alongside the Social Partners. These decisions must not appear to have been taken on high, even if they are the right decisions. They should be reflected upon, adapted, and they should take into account the feelings of those who really know the territory. This seems to me to be vital to the future.

So there you are, *Présidente*, excuse me for having spoken for a long time. I do have one last proposal - very clear, this: I remain convinced that the European Works Councils could be a positive driving force this affair, and it is for this reason that I would like to see the terms of the European Works Councils maintained. They should not be turned into consultative committees.

Thank you.

Ms Tongue:

Thank you very much André.

Can I immediately pass to our last contributor of the day, Dr Dennis Gregory of Ruskin College, Oxford. I would like to ask him to reply to a question which was passed to me earlier today by one of our friends and colleagues here from BMW. It's a very controversial question and I do not believe that we can address it completely today. "How do we equalise wage costs between West and Eastern Europe?"

📖 ***Dr Gregory:***

Thank you very much.

I'd like to make two points about how we might enhance co-operation in the future in the industry. One of them is positive and the second is negative (and I shall try and answer the question as well).

First of all, from what we've heard today and from the communications coming out recently from the Commission on the automobile industry - I think a number of people have expressed this, but it bears repeating - that there is a concern that the Commission has chosen the wrong strategic route to support restructuring and to promote co-operation.

Commissioner Bangemann said this morning that industrial policy was not a sin against the market, and that the European Community's industrial policy was a good policy, which sounded to me like an act of faith.

Mr Perissich followed up and said that in global restructuring there are "no special industries". That's rather a contradiction. His own Communication actually goes out of its way to point out how special and important the motor industry is in Europe. In any event, it stands in stark contrast to the way in which the industry is being targeted and programmed for recovery in the US as other people have said. When President Clinton diverts resources from Star Wars to Car Wars, then he's giving us very important political signals, that the US have been shaken rigid by the Japanese, have now a clear objective of regaining market domination in the autocar industry through technological domination achieved via a clearly focused medium- and long-term strategy for the US car industry. By contrast, we have from Mr Bangemann and Mr Perissich and from others, support for the so-called horizontal approach to industrial policy. It seems to me that we will be left without a vertical industrial policy, without an interventionist industrial policy for the auto industry in Europe, and that, in doing so, we will be out of step from the other two members of the triad, namely the US and Japan, and we will be forever trying to catch up and that is not a position for long-term economic viability.

So, on the negative side, it does seem to me that we have to confront this fundamental contradiction between whether or not we go for some form of a vertical explicit interventionist policy co-ordinated through the Commission, or whether we take the horizontal approach, as being advocated to day. I'll only say on the horizontal approach, what we call in Britain the "blanket approach", and I would simply point out that people go to sleep under blankets.

That brings me neatly onto a second point I wanted to make, which is rather more of a positive one, I think, that is, that it is widely agreed now, not just in the motor industry, and not just in Europe, and certainly in the Scandinavian countries and in the US that future efficiencies, future viabilities and competitiveness, is dependent upon work organisation, and, in that sense, we have some advantages if we develop and promote a social dialogue at every level, but it is notable I think, one of the differences between the

US and Japan is that we have a much more developed participative industrial relations system.

Every country you look at, you see strong signs of participation and involvement. Equally, we now know that any forms of change that are introduced via negotiations and consensus and ultimately agreement, are much more positive than changes which are imposed without agreement, and, equally, there is evidence that productivity increases tend to be higher in traditionally-organised car companies, so there is strong evidence that traditional forms of organisation, traditional industrial relations, systems, actually deliver the goods as far as higher productivity is concerned. What we have to do, and I think it's the future, and it is the job of the Forum or Fora, is to ensure these unique features of European industrial relations systems are turned into a positive competitive advantage insofar as the European industries are concerned, and in that respect I would support other speakers that European works councils could be used to support the development of European works councils.

Moving beyond the consciousness-raising efforts that have been going on up to now, and developing European works councils as a key, company-wide forum that could lock into some ongoing tri-partite dialogue. I think that if we go down this route, and I hope we do, it could be one way that the social partners of the industry achieve a vertically-focused policy intervention despite the Commission's apparent distaste for such departures.

Plainly, the social dialogue does give us some differences between the way in which industries operate in Japan and the US. I think there is plenty of evidence to suggest that we can turn it into a competitive advantage. To come to the question posed about how do we equalise wage costs between Western Europe and Central and Eastern Europe. Trade Unions are already starting on this and working with their counterparts elsewhere in Eastern and Central Europe, very knowledgeable of the fact that at the moment the much much lower wage costs and the desperation of these countries to raise their standards of living is an open door to some form of social dumping, and the best way we can raise to equalise some sort of level playing field, is to develop much better agreements, much higher standards in these particular countries. It certainly will not happen overnight. We need to work towards phased equalisation in terms and conditions of employment.

There has to be some mutual understanding about the way in which investment is put into Central and Eastern Europe and again, I can't think of many better forums than the European works councils and some form of higher-level European tripartite forum to monitor that particular development.

Thank you.

📖 *Ms Tongue:*

Thank you very much.

We are coming to our close. I would just like to thank all our speakers, to apologise that we have not been able to have more of a discussion, but this is the first ever Forum of its kind that the Commission and the Parliament have organised together with all the major players, and clearly we need more time, and we need to go on discussing.

If I may say so, a great deal of convergence has emerged today between the parties here on a range of issues, I believe, particularly on restructuring and the drive for competitivity. There has been a great deal of consensus on training, research and development, Social Dialogue, and partnership issues, and we have heard a range of industrial examples of very good practice that might be emulated.

We also have heard clear demands for the European Commission, and I would add that the Commission must have the support of our national governments if it is to go much beyond the kind of programme that it has before us. We have heard people, very understandably, ask for a long-term specific programme for the car industry, using the model of the United states of America. We have asked for greater co-ordination from the European Commission, which I think has been responded to. We have heard that the kind of Social Dialogue that we have at European level and indeed at plant level should be able to give us a great competitive edge. This is something which the US and Japan do not enjoy to the same level that we do.

Also, if I may say one last word, there is definite support not just to end today with one meeting and one Forum, but to go forward from here, and André Sainjon made one concrete idea, I think it was possibly echoed by other speakers, that there should be technical working groups. One can decide how they might be organised and who might be in them, but certainly they could discuss key issues: funding - Objective 4 and the ADAPT programme that the Commission proposes. One of the things that I find is that the players who are going to have to enact those programmes at regional level have not the structure as yet nor the interface with the Commission to make the best use of those funds. That's a very good reason for having such a working group within the Commission - to discuss those important efforts being made by the Commission to help with the great training challenge within the industry.

Clearly on research and development, on our trading relationships, on Mr Planchon's idea of long-term, low-cost finance for the industry, there should be further discussions. Indeed as regards the components industry in general, which is facing a massive challenge, as yet we have no clear plan at a European level.

So, I hope we can go forward from here, and continue with some kind of permanent though flexible structure.

I just have to respond to Mr Bangemann and Mr Perissich when they pleaded to the European Parliament not to contest the environmental standards that are being proposed by the Commission. Happily we have a democracy of sorts at the European level, so it is precisely our job within the Parliament to have a debate with the Commission on those standards, and I think it is important that we have that debate. Clearly there is disagreement, and yet again it is therefore very good reason why we continue the kind of dialogue that we have here today, because if we all sat round the table more often, then I think we'd get a better understanding, and we wouldn't get in the situation where the Parliament is being asked at the very last moment to back off and reduce its demands - that's a very good reason why we need to go from here and have more groups which I believe will produce a consensus around the issues we've been discussing.

Finally, many many thanks to Mr Wright and Mr Bilson and the support staff within the Commission for all the hard work they have put into this Forum, and a very personal heartfelt thanks to my own assistant, Hilary Lewison, without whom this Forum would not have been possible.

I should like to hand over now to Professor Blanpain of the Catholic University of Leuven, who has very kindly agreed to be with us, and to give his independent summing up of the day's proceedings.

Thank you very much.

FORUM ON THE EUROPEAN AUTOMOBILE INDUSTRY

BRUSSELS - PALAIS DES CONGRÈS - 1 MARCH 1994

INDEPENDENT SUMMARY

PROFESSOR ROGER BLANPAIN
CATHOLIC UNIVERSITY OF LEUVEN

FORUM OF THE EUROPEAN AUTOMOBILE INDUSTRY

BRUSSELS - PALAIS DES CONGRÈS - 1 MARCH 1993

INDEPENDENT SUMMARY

PROFESSOR ROGER BLANPAIN
CATHOLIC UNIVERSITY OF LEUVEN

CONTENTS

Introductory remarks

Summarising not less than 37 speakers and more than 250 pages of notes and documentation inevitably implies that, even when trying to respect the greatest neutrality in the presentation of the different points of view on such a challenging and far-reaching subject like the future of the European automobile industry, **some choices** have to made in discussing **three basic questions** relating to the European automobile industry, namely:

1. Where is the industry at present ?

2. Where is it going ?

3. Can something be done to influence the course of events and if so, what should be done?

"Summing Up" means that one wants to note trends, developments, divergences, convergences, checks and balances, contradictions ... challenges. To put it another way: to try to grasp the most crucial **problems the European automobile industry is confronted with, and evaluate eventual strategies** regarding its future, for the short term as well as the medium and long term.

The importance of the sector

This exercise is even more necessary given the fact that the automobile industry is a significant sector in societal terms:

1. GDP: 2 % of the EU high added value;

2. Employment: more than 11 million employees, directly or indirectly employed;

3. Not only huge enterprises involved, but also thousands of SMEs;

4. New technologies, providing technical impetus and spin-offs, and thriving on dynamic R&D;

5. Infrastructure, needed for an expanding economy in a globalised world;

6. An industry, contributing enormously to the daily mobility of millions of people and enormous amounts of goods.

In short, the automobile industry has **changed and continues to change the face of the Earth**.

Bringing benefits and costs

At the same time, besides benefits, some costs and problems have to be reported. Some of the most important examples relate to:

1. The deterioration of the *environment*;

2. *Congestion* and traffic jams: we are so mobile that we find ourselves increasingly immobile on our motorways;

3. The eventual impact on *regional (growth or) decline*.

An illustrative example

The European automobile industry is also an illustrative example of what is happening to our industries and economies in general since the Berlin wall (1989) came down, China opened up to the world economy, and communication reduced our world to a village.

Like other industries, the automobile sector is sucked up in the **globalisation of the economy**. Our industries, as well as our society in general, are indeed increasingly confronted with:

1. International markets (there are no longer national or regional boundaries for capital, new technologies, production and communication);

2. More and more international products;

3. Shopping worldwide, for the best and the cheapest deal;

4. Producing worldwide;

5. An explosion of networks operating across national and regional boundaries.

The automobile industry is the example *par excellence of the globalisation of our economy, with more and more international products and services, produced by global networks, whereby high* **added value** *is generated in team- and networking between problem finders, -solvers and -brokers: through* **networking** *between "creative* **teamworkers** *and collaborators".*

Massive restructuring

As a consequence, massive restructuring is taking place in many industry and service sectors, caused by a number of "**structural factors**", which compound one another with unprecedented momentum, namely:

1 *New technologies*, which have a tremendous impact on numbers and kinds of jobs;

2 *Modern human resources management*: (international) competition obliging enterprises to do more with less but more motivated "core" people, and also with more "flexibility" in labour contracts, regarding working time, remuneration and the like;

3. *Business re-engineering*[1] of the organisation of work;

4. The *demographic* explosion[2];

5. The *globalisation* of the economy.

Effects on the labour market

Self-evidently, these factors have a tremendous effects on the labour markets, especially that of the private sector, as much the profit as the non-profit sector, and certainly on the automobile labour market. The effect can be summarised in two kinds of jobs and the future they have, namely:

1. Repetitive, *routine jobs* in industry, services and also in management disappear as they are either pushed out by new technologies or as they are exported to low wage[3] regions and countries. This effect leads to **massive unemployment** and with still more jobs to go;

2. *Creative jobs are on the rise.*

---

[1] Business process re-engineering is the fundamental rethinking and radical redesign of business processes to achieve dramatic improvement in critical measures of performance such as cost, quality, service and speed. Re-engineering leads to leaner, flatter organisations; where employees are involved in teamwork with empowered responsibilities and less hierarchy.

[2] Worldwide, 12,500 babies are born every hour, i.e. 300,000 per day. This means that in ten years' time the world population will include 1,000 million more people. It is likely that large proportions of these people will always be candidates for work which is far less paid, and performed under infinitely less favourable working conditions than in our case. Nor must it be forgotten that the EU countries represent barely 5% of the world population, and that this proportion is falling steadily.

[3] Although cost is not the only factor.

Magnitude and importance

It is the importance of the automobile sector and the magnitude of the problems with which the sector is confronted that have inspired the European Parliament, especially MEP Ms. Tongue, and the European Commission to organise this Forum. There was also the explicit desire to ensure that the outcome of the Forum discussions concerning the European automobile industry would produce lessons to be learned for other sectors of industry or services, which are in the same boat as the automotive industry.

A welcomed initiative: advantage or handicap

This Forum on the European automobile industry was welcomed by all participants in the discussion and namely:

1. The European Union: the European Parliament and the Commission;

2. Producers and employers' associations;

3. Suppliers and their associations;

4. Trade Unions;

5. Regional and local authorities;

6. Consumer organisations;

7. Some representatives of the academic community.

So, many important actors were on the platform of the Forum, but undoubtedly not all of them, e.g. the national governments and the insurance companies, were represented at the Forum table. Nevertheless, there were enough participants who engaged in the discussion to have a more or less complete and panoramic view of the responsibilities, problems, strategies and goals involved regarding the future of the European automobile industry.

The Forum agreed that the main question which was to be addressed should be formulated as follows: "**Is belonging to a union an advantage or an handicap for the European automobile industry?**"

A broad and integrated view and approach to tackling that question has been taken by the various participants in the Forum as the following report clearly demonstrates.

RESPONSIBILITIES

Union and Member States

- *Short and long term*

A first point related to the political responsibilities regarding the European automobile industry. This question concentrated on the relationship between the European Union and the Member States in terms of "subsidiarity" as laid down in the Maastricht Treaty. It was largely felt that the *European Union* had to address the *medium- and long-term* strategies regarding the European automobile industry, while *Member States* were judged to be better placed to deal with the *short term*, expressed in terms of *restructuring* (e.g. for reasons of wage costs, involving problems of job security and the like).

- *Horizontal or sectoral policies*

There was a profound exchange of views between different participants in the Forum as to whether the European Union should implement *horizontal or sectoral* policies regarding the industry in general and the automobile sector in particular. The Commission seemed to favour a more global approach, looking at all sectors of industries and services - taking into account the globalisation effect. Others, especially the constructors and the suppliers, pleaded for a more sectoral approach, referring to US and Japanese examples. The Commission insisted however, that a more global approach does not exclude focusing on sectors, it being understood that there are no favours in the drawers for particular sectors. It was noted with pleasure that the Commission promised " a user-friendly interface".

Constructors and suppliers

All agreed that it is the main responsibility of the constructors and the suppliers to *restructure* the sector, however with more co-ordination, working together with the other parties involved.

Trade Unions

Trade Unions reported that they were mainly looking for real *partnerships*.

Regional and local authorities

Regional and local authorities were especially pondering over the *decline in the regions and the localities*, due to the restructuring in the automobile sector, and its effect on jobs, as well as over the possibilities for the automobile industry to foster *growth*.

Consumers

Consumers were looking for an even *deal* for the customers.

Academics

The academic world indicated the need for more vision and research-based action.

"The overall message which came out of the Forum was the prevailing need and objective for all actors, the European Union, the Member States, regional and local authorities included, as well as the manufacturers, suppliers, Trade Unions, consumers and the academic community to work together."

POLICIES

A broad consensus emerged from the discussion, namely that the formulation of problems, strategies and goals had to be examined from that point of view and geared toward the competitivity of the European automobile industry. This consensus involves not less than 10 headings:

1   Competitivity

All participants in the discussion agreed on the need for the auto mobile industry to be *competitive*: to be able to compete in the world market, and de facto to engage in worldwide *benchmarking*. The *consumers* indicated that there should be even more competitivity, in a sense all the way for the benefit of the consumers in particular and society at large in general. But this was certainly not the opinion of everyone involved, especially of *constructors and suppliers*, especially in view of the relationship to other automotive producing regions and/or nations, e.g. Japan. The *Trade Unions* insisted that competition should be done on the basis of the *training* of employees, increased *partnership* as well as job security, all of which the Trade Unions claimed were prerequisites for quality products. *Producers and suppliers* insisted also on the need to *lower costs* and to introduce *more flexibility, among others* regarding labour matters, in order to be able to compete effectively.

2   Globalisation

Globalisation of the industry was widely accepted, not only as unavoidable, but also projected by the Commission as an *explicit goal for the European automobile industry*. The Commission underlined that the European industry was yet not global enough, and that one has to act globally in order not to lose jobs at home. Since this view leads inevitably to *restructuring in the sector*, the Commission was urged by quite a number of participants to provide funds to that end, especially to provide for *training* and facilities to mitigate the effects of *redundancies*.

3   Single market

A strong argument was made for completing the single market as soon as possible e.g., regarding regulations, taxes, exchange rates and low-cost financing to the industry included. The European Union, it was stressed, should ensure *regulatory stability* and especially speedy and swift but also *consistent action* regarding emissions and selective distribution.

4   Reciprocity

Although a global market was recognised as a crucial goal, an urgent call was made for full *reciprocity* between different world regions. There was a plea, especially from the constructors, to apply the agreement with Japan not only with intelligence but also with firmness. Efficient external trade policies against dumping and pirate parts were requested. Regarding *low-wage countries*, the suppliers declared that "extremely low salaries and the virtual absence of social cover costs will significantly impact the European Market" if uncontrolled. Reciprocity, the suppliers stated, will need to be considered.

5   Regional / Local

Regional and local aspects were repeatedly stressed. Indeed, restructuring in the European automobile industry can have a heavy impact on regions / localities and may add to increasing *discrepancies* in income and wealth between regions and groups in society at large. The important role of the Community was underlined, especially in the area of *restructuring*, where the Community should help. It was however equally indicated that the automobile industry can and should help to renovate regions and localities. Within this framework, the role of regional and local authorities in the "auto regions" was stressed: there was a plea for more integrated *innovation programmes*, for the establishment of *network cultures*, which should also operate across boundaries as well for *social dialogue*. It was only when those measures were successfully implemented, so it was argued, "that *training initiatives* can be really meaningful".

6   Environment

Some of the participants insisted especially on the importance of the environmental aspects related to the European automobile industry and among others on the following:

a.   An enhanced role for R&D, not only regarding the *protection* of the environment, but also geared toward a better use of *energy;*

b.   A possible role for (increased) *taxes;*

c.   The use of *recycling;*

d.   The elimination & decrease of *noise;*

e.   The importance of *public transport.*

Regarding these environmental issues the *automobile industry* asked for a *balance* between the efforts of all actors to be maintained.

7　Vocational training

A need for an enhanced and new approach regarding vocational training was stressed by all participants in the Forum as:

a.　a means to be *competitive*;

b.　the way for lasting "*employability*".

Education and permanent training should be more geared towards teamwork, innovation and creativity (rather than to repetitive jobs), and this together with more empowerment of the employees and less hierarchy in the enterprises. It is a mission for all involved to see that employees and managers, self-employed included, receive the type of training which best equips them for creative work, so that products of world-class value can be made and services delivered.

The *Trade Unions* insisted that there should be either *training or a levy* paid by enterprises in the absence of adequate training. Training should also contribute, they said, to the promotion of *free movement of workers*. All participants in the discussion underlined that training should also be geared towards other jobs, other sectors, directed at *new activities*, while local and regional actors and levels should be more involved. The Commission was asked to provide *guidance* regarding training by indicating training targets and mechanisms.

8　Reorganisation of work

Reorganisation of work was equally addressed as a way to:

a.　promote *competitivity* (considering that the Japanese have superior production organisation methods);

b.　redistribute available work, including flexible arrangements.

In this context the Trade Unions furthered their request for *lowering working time* by referring to the VW arrangement in Germany[4]. In this area one was obviously looking for "*best practice*" from which everyone can learn from each other.

---

[4]　A four-day week instead of five, with a substantial cut in pay, in order to save 30,000 jobs.

9   Research and Development

Everyone agreed that R&D is enormously important (*la nerf de la guerre*) in furthering of the European automobile industry. There was wide agreement:

a.   that R&D should be undertaken more *globally*;

b.   in a spirit of *co-operation*. This should be fostered by the European Union and also in a user friendly way;

c.   that the *best practices* should be circulated;

d.   that more should be done to match *overseas investment* in R&D and to promote *horizontal research programmes*.

10 Social dialogue

Finally, the need for more social dialogue and co-operation at various levels was underlined, including regional, local levels, as well as at the level of the enterprise. Trade Unions insisted upon adequate *information and consultation* for the employees and asked that their representatives should be treated as "fully-fledged partners". In this framework a plea was made for the establishment of *European works councils*, which would give substance to the idea of partnership.

FINAL SUMMARY

Summarising strategies, goals and policies the following points and trends can be thus retained:

- competitivity
- globalisation
- enhancing the single market
- installing reciprocity in the world of the auto mobile industry, thus ensuring "a fair level playing field"
- regional and local inputs
- environmental requirements
- vocational training for creative and new jobs
- reorganisation of work to remain competitive and redistribute available work
- R&D: more; more horizontal ; more co-operation
- social dialogue and co-operation at all levels by all actors involved, while respecting (local) traditions and moving towards more competitive advantage.

Message from the Forum

The message coming out of this Forum is loud and clear: **there is a strong belief in the future of the European automobile industry**.

But at the same time there was agreement that Europe can only win:

a.   if everyone works *together*: no false wars between various industries of transport;

b.   if there is *co-operation* at all levels in full partnership.

It was widely felt that there have never been so many *challenges*, which have to be tackled with *creative and forward looking solutions*.

Belonging to a Union should definitely be an advantage for the European automobile industry, everyone agreed, provided everyone can work together.

Here the need for a **vision** beyond the short and the medium term was underlined: a vision directed at the 21st century.

Much of the Forum, so it was also concluded, contained **lessons for others sectors of industry and/or services**.

As one participant put it: *dreams are not always an illusion - they sometimes come true*.

Finally, the wish was expressed to evaluate the follow-up of this Forum on European automobile industry by way of another Forum in the not-too-distant future.

FORUM ON THE EUROPEAN AUTOMOBILE INDUSTRY

BRUSSELS - PALAIS DES CONGRÈS - 1 MARCH 1994

AN ASSESSMENT

MS. CAROLE TONGUE, MEP
EUROPEAN PARLIAMENT
RAPPORTEUR ON THE CAR INDUSTRY

The Forum on the future of the European car industry brought together for the first time on an equal basis all the interested parties in the European car industry. In the Palais des Congrès in Brussels on March 1st, under the joint auspices of the European Commission and the European Parliament, some 370 delegates gathered together and heard during the course of the day, through four carefully formulated workshops, how the car industry is facing increasing competition and challenges. The European Commission and other EU institutions came under pressure to develop a more coherent and better financed strategy for the European car industry.

The Background

As production processes change and systems become leaner, car workers need new skills and are required to work in different ways. These radical changes clearly require new partnerships and new understanding between suppliers and manufacturers, and between manufacturers and their whole workforce.

The European Commission, in its recent Communication, recognises that the survival of the auto industry depends on a good restructuring process. This means successful adaptation of the workforce to new production procedures. It also means job losses. The concern of the European Parliament is that this should be resourced and managed well and humanely: hence the way forward lies with restructuring being managed through Social Dialogue and partnership. Public policy should assist the process through training funds, Objective 4 and ADAPT, but with better resources.

The Bottom Line

The main message from the conference was how dialogue should go forward and here Ms. Tongue, Rapporteur for the European Parliament on the car industry, and on whose recommendation the Forum had been created, made a strong plea to the Commission for a sectoral approach to the car industry. With 8 million jobs directly and indirectly attributable to the car industry, it was essential, she said, to have long-term, specific programmes. There should be greater co-ordination between the competent DGs and the Commission, and, most importantly, there must be support for Social Dialogue when developing public policy for the industry.

The Significance of Human Resources

In Workshop 1, the use of human resources was highlighted, as well as how new relationships could be enlarged, how important it is to ensure that people are respected and that any partnership is not an imposition. The Trade Unions emphasised that Social Dialogue and high quality training was imperative for restructuring, and that employers should be obliged to train or pay a levy in the event of no training. The importance of dialogue was stressed to create a new relationship between suppliers and manufacturers. There was a call for long-term, low-cost finance programmes from the European Union, and a query as to why in the EC-Japan Accord there was no agreement on components presently being made by the European manufacturers. In addition, Union representatives explained that as well as wanting to maintain the present levels of employment they wanted to make their contribution to improved competitivity.

The Role of the Regions

Workshop 3, dealing with the regional aspect of industry, emphasised the need for a stronger networking system, with help from the EU so that car regions can interrelate to far greater mutual benefit and work towards a clear sectoral policy. Sharing ideas and experiences on how best to manage restructuring at a regional level to benefit the whole community was seen as crucial.

Strengthening Partnership

In her closing remarks to Workshop 4, Ms. Tongue pointed out how much support for a Social Dialogue had been emphasised by speakers from all workshops. From Workshop 4, there had emerged a clear vision on partnerships and dialogue at all levels in a formal structured way. Technical working groups need to be set up by the Commission creating a new social partnership between the social partners and the Commission to discuss issues such as:

- Funding for Objective 4 and the ADAPT programme;

- Research and Development;

- Trading relationships;

- Long-term / low-cost finance, and

- Components.

This will ensure that all public policy has both the input and the support of the social partners. This is the key to its success. It is essential that the momentum created by this Forum is not lost and that a solid partnership is created between the social partners and the Commission. Thus all parties involved in this vital industrial sector will benefit into the twenty-first century.

FORUM ON THE EUROPEAN AUTOMOBILE INDUSTRY

BRUSSELS - PALAIS DES CONGRÈS - 1 MARCH 1994

ANNEXES

The Automobile Industry - Current Situation,
Challenges, Strategy for the Future and Proposals for Action

(1) The Current Situation

The global picture

The European automobile industry is a key industry in the EU employing directly more than 1.8 million people in the supply and manufacturing chain. An additional 1.8 million people are employed in the distribution and repair sector. Indirectly the livelihood of many more citizens depend on the success of the industry. The industry accounts for nearly 2% of total GDP in the EU.

The automotive industry is a global industry dominated by three large trading areas - the EU, the US and Japan. Traditional EU manufacturers retain a dominant position on the EU market (84 % market share in 1993) but are present to only a small degree on the markets of Japan (EU exports amounted to only 2% of the total Japanese market in 1993) and the US (EU exports were only 2% of the US market in 1993).

The "Big Three" US car makers occupy 74% of a US market roughly equivalent in terms of size to the EU market but are barely present on the markets of Japan (less than 1% in 1993 with the bulk of the sales being sales by Japanese transplants). US exports to the EU are minimal (0.5% in 1993). It is important to note however that for the first time in many years the "Big Three" gained market share in the US market in 1993 (almost 2% gain principally at the expense of Japanese makes).

By contrast Japanese manufacturers dominate totally the market in Japan (supplying 97% of the market in 1993) and occupy significant market shares in the US (23% in 1993, a drop of 1% from 1992) and in the EU (11.4% in 1993). These large market shares are underpinned increasingly by a growing volume of transplant production. Thus out of the 11.4% market share in the EU, 3% were sales by transplants. By contrast EU investment in these two markets is relatively small; it is only within the last 2 years for example that two specialist EC constructors have announced their intent to build vehicles in the US . No EU car company produces in Japan. US car companies have of course been present in the EU market for many years (Ford and GM collectively supply about a quarter of the EU market) but have no manufacturing presence in Japan.

Reflecting these relative degrees of market penetration and despite the increasing importance of the transplants, Japan has run substantial trade surpluses with the EU and the US both in terms of vehicles as well as parts for repairing vehicles. The total automotive trade surplus with the EU is currently in the order of ECU 9 billion (some 30% of the total) whilst the US trade deficit in autos and auto parts with Japan is around $30 billion annually.

The short-term market outlook in the EU

The current market environment in the EU is one of considerable difficulty. In 1993 the EU market for cars and light utility vehicles fell by 15.9% to 11.74 million vehicles, the largest year on year fall ever recorded. With the very strong concentration of EU production on the EU market the consequence of such a drastic downturn in Europe for the EU industry has been serious in terms of production cutbacks, stock build-up, capacity underutilisation, plant closures, widespread financial losses, short-time working and employment losses. Nearly 70,000 jobs were lost just in manufacturing in 1993 and in 1994 already announced plans by the producers suggest that there will be further losses of nearly 40,000 jobs leaving a total industry manufacturing employment of 900,000. The downturn in the market has been passed through to component suppliers whose prices have been under considerable pressure from manufacturers pressing to reduce the overall cost of production to reduce the break-even point in a declining market. In the short-term this market outlook will not substantially improve. There will be either stagnation or only very slow growth in the EU in 1994 with some variations by Member State. Growth is not expected to resume before 1995 . This situation contrasts with the buoyant US market which grew by 8% in 1993 and which is forecast to expand further in 1994.

(2) **The Challenges Ahead**

Longer term growth prospects in the EU market are good and it is expected that by the year 2000 the annual market should rise to more than 15 million units. Improved economic conditions in Europe will underpin the expansion in the market. It has to be recognised, however, that with the rise in the vehicle parc environmental problems will increase. Indeed it cannot be overlooked that many urban areas in Europe have reached near saturation as far as car mobility is concerned. At the same time the consumer continues to choose the car as the optimum means of transport best suited to his needs and requires products of ever increasing quality which are safe, environmentally friendly, reliable, cheap to purchase and maintain.

In effect the desire for personal mobility has to be set against the nuisance of pollution and traffic congestion. This dilemma can only be resolved by the industry developing cleaner cars and by governments improving performance in spatial planning as well as improving infrastructures including enhanced traffic management through the use of telematics and innovative road pricing schemes. The management of these issues within the framework of an overall policy designed to support the competitiveness of the industry represents one of the key challenges to governments and industry.

The future of the EU industry is to a very large degree dependent on its ability to restructure in order to improve its competitivity by reducing costs and improving the quality, innovativeness and environmental performance of its products and to meet the global competitive challenges ahead. These include the full opening up of the EU market by the end of 1999 to competition from Japanese companies which is mitigated, for the time being, by the sharp rise in the value of the yen, the arrival of new competitors on the scene notably from Korea and the revival of the US industry. Not only is the EU producers' home market under threat, but it is becoming increasingly difficult for them to compete successfully on third markets. This is all the more pertinent in view of the good growth prospects in new markets such as Eastern Europe, Latin America, Asia and China.

Compared to US and Japanese manufacturers, EU automobile producers are under-represented in markets other than their home markets. The ability to create and develop a strong position in these markets often requires local production capacity to be built up close to the market in question so as to be able to supply it with products adapted to its specific needs. Where the alternative to producing locally in such markets is to abandon it altogether, the development of such facilities can protect high value added jobs in the EU and increase the financial stability of its manufacturers.

Restructuring amongst the EU's component suppliers is equally vital, the more so in the light of the increasing degree of outsourcing of systems and component production to suppliers. In the car of the future it is likely that at least 60% of the value added will be supplied outside the manufacturer. A considerable handicap in terms of productivity has to be overcome (generally estimated to be in the region of 30%) in order that suppliers' are in a position to match the performance reached by those of its competitors notably in Japan. This restructuring process is only just getting underway in Europe.

Increasing competitiveness in terms of quality and cost of production requires improvements in the qualifications of the labour force of the companies concerned. This means adapting the labour force to new production systems and industrial changes through vocational training programmes designed to develop teamworking, multiskilling and flexibility. These new requirements apply throughout the production chain; a crucial element will be the development of close partnership relations between suppliers and manufacturers and between manufacturers and distributors aimed at creating new "lean" structures adapted to modern production and marketing. Such systems are dependent on the quality of human resources to manage and implement them.

For those who will be obliged to leave the industry retraining programmes need to be devised in order to offer the real prospect of employment in a different sector.

(3) Strategy

As set out in the White Paper on Growth, Competitiveness and Employment, new approaches need to be taken to promoting growth in a sustainable way responding to the twin challenges of achieving a higher intensity of employment and a lower intensity of the consumption of energy and natural resources while at the same time improving the quality of life through the development of new innovative products based on clean technologies. The best way for the automobile industry to integrate into this future environment is to develop competitive, clean and "intelligent" cars according to modern development, process and production methods supported by a highly qualified, multiskilled and flexible labour force. In essence the objective is to develop "**Clean, lean-produced, intelligent, quality, value** " cars for the year 2000 and beyond.

Such cars would be competitive world class products and would thereby permit EU manufacturers to regain the market share they once occupied on third markets notably the US. The industry must have as its objective market expansion world wide and not limited regional aims which are not sustainable in the long run.

The primary responsibility for effecting the changes necessary to fulfil these objectives rests with industry. The strategy requires the industry to take the lead in developing close collaborative relations within companies through cooperative working structures between managers, team leaders and workers. It also requires partnership relations along the whole supply chain - supplier/manufacturer, manufacturer/distributor, distributor/consumer. The implementation of such relationships is clearly the responsibility of the industry. The public authorities must create a supportive business environment based on open and competitive markets which will encourage manufacturers to undertake the necessary actions to improve their competitiveness. It is the role of the Union and its Member States to ensure that such an environment is achieved in accordance with Article 130 of the Maastricht Treaty. The Union can assist this process by facilitating the smooth functioning of the internal market in a competitive environment, by ensuring that horizontal policy instruments are applied to speed up the adjustment of the industry to industrial change, to encourage cooperation between undertakings and to foster joint research as well as a better exploitation of the results of such programmes.

The profound changes which are needed, first and foremost those in the sphere of human resources, require a relationship of partnership and trust between management and labour and the full attention of the authorities. Dialogue between the partners is both a democratic necessity and an efficient way of mobilising the entire automobile industry. According to Article 118 B of the Treaty, the Commission has the task of promoting this dialogue.

(4) Proposals

(a) Internal Market

The further development of the internal market will continue to have an important impact on the car industry's competitiveness. It is essential first of all that continuing vigilance be applied to ensure that no new barriers are introduced which would disrupt the operation of the internal market. Further efforts must be applied also to ensure that any remaining barriers, for example in the technical area, are eliminated. Finally new regulatory initiatives must give a sufficient lead-time to industry to enable it to forward plan and make the appropriate adjustments to comply with new rules.

(i) A competitive market

The provision of a competitive market environment is a precondition for creating competitive industries in the Union.

In its approach towards cooperation in the motor vehicles sector, the Commission takes into account the larger dimension of the internal market and the fact that the motor vehicle market has become a world market. Strict conditions may be applied to collaborative ventures amongst assemblers to avoid spill-over effects negative to competition in other areas of the business partners concerned. In the component sector the Commission takes full account of the fact that co-operation and concentration often have the largest impact in terms of reducing costs and improving competitiveness in a key sector which is trailing its competitors in this domain.

State Aids continue to be decided upon under the Aid Framework for the motor vehicle industry. The Commission has approved the grant of aid where it has been shown that the aid has been in proportion to the problems it seeks to solve and that the aid is compatible with the overall interests of the Union. The Commission will continue to monitor the level of aid granted to the industry closely in order to ensure that investment risks remain with private operators and that the competitiveness of the Community industry is not distorted by unfair competition. It will ensure that all cases of notified aids are dealt with expeditiously.

(ii) The distribution system

Regulation 123/85 on selective and exclusive distribution has provided a structured framework against which motor vehicle distribution arrangements have been drawn up. The aim of the Regulation has been to establish a fair balance of interests between all actors in the distribution chain (manufacturers, distributors and parts producers) while ensuring that consumers benefit overall from the system.

The Commission has begun reviewing the functioning of the Regulation, which expires in June 1995, in conjunction with all interested parties. The Commission recognises that in order to provide important planning stability for investment in the distribution chain, which employs some 1.1 million people in the Community a decision should be reached quickly on how the Regulation should be applied in the future.

In its review, the Commission will take account of the following elements :-

- the extent to which the Regulation contributes to improving distribution and increasing inter and intra-brand competition;

- the progress in the functioning of the internal market in the automotive sector and the impact of the Regulation in this regard;

- the balance of interests between the different parties concerned (constructors/distributors; constructors/parts producers; consumers);

- the need to foster close partnership relations between all elements of the distribution chain in order to improve industrial efficiency and competitiveness in the automotive sector as a whole and preserve employment notably in small and medium sized enterprises;

- the contribution of the selective and exclusive distribution system to the efficient management of the arrangement between Japan and the EU on trade in automobiles; the efficient management of this arrangement must not be weakened in any way.

(iii) <u>Harmonisation of taxes</u>

A major step towards reducing divergences in taxation between Member States was made in 1993 when the implementation of a minimum VAT rate of 15% and the abolition of higher VAT rates came into effect . Remaining differences in taxes on motor vehicles are in certain cases substantial and it cannot be denied that these disparities affect the overall business environment for the car industry and have a negative impact on the internal market. The next stage, foreseen for 1994, will be to make proposals aimed at harmonising the structure of car circulation taxes to take account of environmental factors. At a later stage the Commission will examine the possibility of further harmonisation related to circulation taxes. As regards car registration taxes where the greatest disparities exist between the tax regimes of different Member States, the Commission will ensure that these taxes are compatible with the proper functioning of the internal market.

(iv) <u>Improvement of Vehicle safety</u>

The development of new passive and active standards for vehicle construction represent one of the key elements in the road safety system (driver, vehicle, infrastructure).New proposals aimed at improving the crashworthiness testing procedures of vehicles will be proposed by the Commission shortly, which will ensure that the highest attainable standards are put in place consistent with scientific and technical developments. The Commission is also anxious to see improvements in coach safety and will examine proposals, inter alia, with regard to the technical aspects of safety belts.

These proposals will be made within the framework of the European whole vehicle type approval system which has been in force since 1993 on an optional basis. The system becomes mandatory in 1996. The Commission will hold a conference at the end of 1994 to discuss experiences in the implementation of the system. Preparatory work is continuing with a view to setting up an information network for exchanging information between type approval authorities.

(v) <u>Measures to promote environmental sustainability</u>

The main environmental problems to be tackled are air pollution caused by car emissions, emissions of carbon dioxide stemming from the consumption of fuel, noise, congestion and other nuisances in urban areas and solid waste from the scrapping of used vehicles.

Most progress has been made on reducing car emissions. The Commission has taken the lead in setting advanced environmental standards. The approach has been to adopt the highest standards consistent with the technology available while ensuring a stable predictable policy environment for manufacturers to plan the introduction of cleaner cars. The latter is all the more important in view of the significant cost in new facilities and tooling for manufacturers arising from each stage to reduce car emissions. The draft directive on car emissions COM(92)572 which sets new standards from 1996 was the subject of a common position in the Council in December 1993. The proposals would lead to a reduction of 50% or more in most air polluting emissions compared to levels set in 1991.

A key innovation in this proposal is the setting down of a framework of possible measures to be taken in the year 2000 to reduce emissions. The cost effectiveness of each measure will be assessed prior to the formulation of the Commission's proposal which is due to be made at the end of 1994. In this context the Commission views very favourably the recently launched Auto-Oil research programme set up in conjunction with the automobile industry (ACEA) and the petroleum industry (EUROPIA) to examine the contribution that reformulated fuels and improved engine technologies could make to reducing emissions in the year 2000.

In 1994 the Commission will be putting forward proposals to reduce CO_2 emissions for motor vehicles as part of a strategy to reduce emissions from the transport sector as a whole. With respect to CO_2 emissions from motor vehicles a fiscal approach towards reducing such emissions would seem to be the most promising approach, combined perhaps with an upwards harmonisation of the minimum rates of fuel taxes. Proposals relating to noise measurement and tyre rolling noise will be made in 1994.

The Commission intends to launch a dialogue with the industry aimed at addressing the interaction between industrial policy and the Union's environmental objectives. In this context, an important element in meeting the environmental challenge will be for the car industry to concentrate its activities into products, systems and services more favourable to the environment, both for private use and for public transport.

(b) EC policy in the field of structural interventions and human resources

Interventions aimed at speeding up the adjustment of industry to structural changes are one of the key elements necessary to ensure the competitiveness of industry. For this reason the Union's horizontal structural policy instruments have a key role to play towards facilitating change and making it socially acceptable inter alia in the automobile industry and, in accordance with Article 123 of the Treaty, facilitating the adaptation of workers to industrial changes and to changes in production systems particularly through vocational training and retraining.

Since coming into existence, the European Regional Development Fund (ERDF) and the European Social Fund (ESF) have supported productive investment and vocational training to various degrees in industries concentrated in the regions eligible for such support. The automotive industry has been a beneficiary of such actions. Support has been given in the form of investment aid to encourage productive investment in major projects in the automobile sector located in Objective 1 regions[1] ; in addition investments in infrastructures directly related to production have helped to create a sound basis for industrial development. In Objective 2 areas[2], additional amounts have been used for direct investment support. In these regions, the Commission has also concentrated its efforts on improving the general competitive environment of industries. This category of expenditure includes the provision of services to enterprises, RTD and technical training. The industry has also benefitted from loans granted by the European Investment Bank[3].

The resources available to the Union for structural interventions have been considerably enhanced; at a Union level more than ECU 154 billion has been set aside for structural interventions for 1994-1999.

A major innovation has been the adoption of horizontal policy instruments applicable throughout the Union aimed at anticipating the consequences of industrial change and changes in production systems of workers in employment. These are of particular relevance to the automobile industry most of whose vehicle and component manufacturing facilities are outside Objective 1 & 2 regions. In this context training and retraining measures should focus on two areas which are the keys to structural adjustment and competitiveness and which are highly important to the car industry.

-   Training based on the introduction, use and development of new or improved production methods.

-   Training reflecting the need for SMEs to adapt to new forms of co-operation with major companies, particularly with regard to subcontracting.

---

[1]   Regions whose development is lagging behind.

[2]   Regions seriously affected by industrial decline.

[3]   Over the last 5 years total amounts for direct investment support in objective 1 and 2 regions have been substantially in excess of ECU 300 million and loans granted by the EIB have been around ECU 600 million per annum. Under the Community Framework on State Aid to the Motor Vehicle Industry, Member States have granted ECU 5 billion since 1989.

Three new instruments have been created which will be of particular relevance for the automobile sector in this context :-

-   Objective 4 of the Structural Funds which is designed to adapt the workforce to structural change. Spending under Community Support Frameworks outside Objective 1 regions can reach more than ECU 2 billion in the 1994-9 period, where the majority of car and car component manufacturing plants are located. Significant further funding will be possible in Objective 1 regions.

-   The new Community Initiative ADAPT, which will be concentrated on Objective 4 actions throughout the Union inter alia on cooperative actions across frontiers; the amount allocated to this initiative has been set at ECU 1.4 billion of which 1 billion is to be spent outside Objective 1 regions.

-   The Community Initiative programme for SMEs (PME) (ECU 1 billion) which offers the possibility of reinforcing the capacity for actions in favour of small and medium sized enterprises in a networking approach. ECU 200 million has been set aside for regions outside Objective 1.

The principal aim of these new measures is to strengthen employment and job qualifications and to anticipate the consequences of industrial change and changes in production systems on workers in employment, and address future skill needs. Efforts by constructors and suppliers to work together could be of particular interest; these companies should take advantage of these important new possibilities to improve competitiveness. Furthermore the new measures reinforce actions in the fields of quality strategies, management and organisation, diffusion of RDt results, services to industries and improve the access of SMEs to finance and credit.

In parallel with these new measures the Community action programmes such as Comett and Force on vocational training run by the Task Force Human Resources have continued to facilitate the transfer of innovation and know-how on training in industry. It is now envisaged that a transnational network including automotive companies will be established in the framework of the Force-programme, to ensure a wider and more efficient dissemination on a multisectoral basis of the experiences gained from existing vocational training programmes.

Although the Community action programmes come to the end of their current life cycle at the end of 1994, a Commission Communication to the Council (COM(93)686 Final) has been made for a new action programme for the implementation of a Community vocational training policy (LEONARDO da Vinci). This will take forward the achievements of the current programmes in a single framework and will continue to provide opportunities for industry to innovate on a transnational basis in the field of training and human resources development.

(c) **Research and Technological Development**

The White Paper clearly identified that Research and Technological Development has a vital role to play in assuring the future competitiveness of EU industry. In addition it identified that a key element of a strategic microeconomic policy is a significant reorientation of basic research towards areas of particular relevance to the sustainable development model and secondly, the need to speed up the incorporation of the results of basic research into marketable innovations.

These considerations are of particular relevance to the automobile industry which is facing massive challenges in terms of improvements in systems to design, develop and produce new cars, the need to incorporate new materials and more electronic componentry in vehicles, the need for improvements in technology spurred by environmental and safety requirements, and the interaction with road and transport infrastructures.

It is essential therefore that public authorities support the research and development efforts of the industry; the Union for its part has a key role to play in stimulating **joint research and technological development** between companies within the industry as well as on a wider **multisectoral** basis.

It is vital that these efforts do not lag behind those of Japan and the US. In the US for example, a high political priority has been given to building a prototype of a New Generation Vehicle (NGV). This consists of an industry-led sectoral effort to harness the resources of government (including defence laboratories) and industry through ad hoc research consortia carrying out work on technologies with short to long term applications[1]. While European structures are different the research objectives in terms of producing a "clean, lean produced, intelligent" car are not. What is required is a clear focus of all the European actors involved.

The investment in research and development by the European automobile industry is immense; ECU 4 billion annually is directed at precompetitive and generic research. Under the Third Framework Programme around 550 million ECU, approximately 10% of the total amounts expended, were granted to projects with potential application or benefit to the EU automobile industry.

For the Fourth Framework Programme from 1994-8, which is in the course of being finalised in the Council and the European Parliament, the Commission has proposed a significant total funding package amounting to ECU 13.1 billion. The focus will remain on generic, precompetitive research with a multi-sectoral impact. However, there will be a greater selectivity and concentration of Community actions and a closer integration of Community and national activities including those of EUREKA. The programme also envisages improved access to programmes for SMEs, a feature of particular importance to the automobile industry when the component suppliers will be increasingly required to assume greater technological competences in the light of the restructuring of the value chain.

The automobile industry has proposed to concentrate on research on underlying technologies, on areas impacting the cost structure of the industry and on areas with a significant environmental impact. The following areas of the Fourth Framework Programme respond to these needs :-

The specific programme on **industrial technologies** will continue to be a major focus of research of value to industry with concentration on key technologies which industry has helped identify. It will address the conception of vehicles and the integration of systems, production, improvements in propulsive systems, the reduction of environmental impacts and increasing safety.

The programme on **clean and efficient energy technologies** will also address questions of strategic interest for the future of car research in the field of the further reduction of polluting emissions by conventional engines/catalytic systems, which will be co-ordinated with the Auto-Oil industry project, and will also examine the evolution of fuel properties. Community research aimed at achieving a technological breakthrough in the critical components for electrically-propelled vehicles, such as batteries and fuel cells, will also receive increased Community funding.

Important benefits for the industry are expected from research in **information technologies,** in particular from activities in the field of computer-integrated manufacturing and engineering, open microprocessors and micro-electronics for motor vehicles (MICROMOBILE). Advanced **Communication** technologies and services can assist design, maintenance and other applications, which can improve the competitiveness of the automobile industry. Further support in developing "intelligent vehicles" will be given via **Telematics** which will also support the action of advanced Road Traffic Management Systems as a continuation of the DRIVE programme.

Due to the challenge for industrial and public partners to abate all kinds of pollution created by the use of road transport, the research programme on the **environment,** especially its part focused on technologies, is deemed to have significant applications for developing those technologies which

---

[1]   The Commission is concerned in particular about access of EU companies to this programme, whether they be automobile constructors or component producers, and has pointed out to the US government and industry that US companies with a manufacturing and research base are active participants in EU framework programmes. It is in the interest of all parties that comparable and effective market access is guaranteed in this area.

have a direct bearing on the content of other specific programmes, such as the disposal of waste, recycling and the reduction of effluents and emissions in manufacturing processes.

Directly in the sphere of interest for the automobile industry, the programme for **Research in the field of Transport** will promote actions focused on the interface with other transport modes as well as the improvement of road transport safety, and will lead to a better integration of road transport in an efficient global transport system. The car industry has also shown interest in the targeted **socio-economic programme** .

It is important to ensure that the research needs, as perceived by the various industries, are channelled into planning and management of Community RTD activities in a coherent and efficient way. Dialogues with user-group panels, producers and component suppliers, enabling the broad spectrum of automotive research interests to be absorbed into the R&D content of specific programmes already occur but need to be enhanced further within appropriate user-friendly frameworks. To this end, the Commission will closely collaborate with specialised industrial panels in order to respond to problems identified by such groups with a view to ensuring a better utilisation of the specific research programmes.

Equally importantly, the Commission will pay particular attention to the fact that certain areas of research co-operation of interest to the automobile industry can cut across different activities of the framework programme, and can cause difficulties in applications and funding. The level of internal co-ordination and consultation between individual programmes of research is being enhanced significantly to ensure a more coherent approach towards integrated projects covering a number of different programmes.

It is envisaged that the next call for proposals in the framework of the new specific programmes will be published towards the end of 1994. This will ensure a continuity of support for the research efforts of the automobile industry into 1995.

(d) External Trade Policy Environment ("volet externe")

(i) EU Market

More than eighty different makes of car compete on the EU market reflecting its high degree of openness. This is reinforced by the policy of freedom of investment and circulation of goods within the EU, and finally by the wide extent of preferential access granted to a wide variety of countries.

Given the economic importance of the sector, and the openness of the market, it is particularly sensitive to disruptions arising from imports of finished or semi-finished products. Special attention therefore continues to be given by the Union to avoiding trade distortions or other actions which might disrupt the market.

- Avoidance of Unfair Practices

Dumping or unjustified subsidies can have serious injurious effects on EU producers. In the case of relatively low-cost producing countries, unfair pricing could add to the already existing pricing advantage and would jeopardise the ability of the EU producers to compete at the lower end of the market. In February 1994 the General Affairs Council agreed measures defining the EU's import regime and new rules for commercial defense instruments. As a result of this decision the EU now has a set of instruments which are more efficient than before for dealing with unfair trade practices.

- Avoidance of Market Disruption

In the automobile sector an arrangement was achieved with Japan in July 1991. It aims in particular at the progressive opening of the EU market to Japanese exports of cars and LCVs over a transitional period ending on 31 December 1999, while avoiding the market disruptions that could result from such exports. The stability that follows from these conditions will be favourable to the restructuring of the industry, and thus to its aim of achieving adequate levels of international competitiveness by the end of 1999.

The co-operation of the Japanese authorities in monitoring their exports during the transitional period aims at ensuring, firstly, that the opening of the five previously restricted markets (France, Italy, Spain, Portugal, United Kingdom) will be conducted in a progressive way, taking into account the various market developments. Particularly important is the need for Japanese manufacturers to avoid any targeting of these specific markets through excessive concentration of the sales of their products manufactured in the EU. Secondly, the monitoring of exports to the Union is conducted in such a way that, while ensuring an adequate supply to non-restricted markets, the volume of sales of traditional EU producers will not be unduly affected. This will ensure that these producers are able during the transitional period to generate the cash flow required to pay for the restructuring and adaptation costs necessary to enhance their competitiveness in time for when the market is fully opened up at the end of the decade.

The consultations held so far between the Commission and MITI, in particular those held in 1993, show that reasonable compromises can be reached even in exceptionally unfavourable circumstances such as those presently prevailing in the car market. In September 1993 the forecast of Japanese exports to the EU for 1993 was revised to 980,000, a reduction of 18.4 % on the 1992 figure, on the basis of demand estimated to fall by 15.9 %, to 11.73 million units for 1993. These forecast figures exactly reflected the actual results in 1993. The overall market declined by 15.9 % to reach 11.739 million units, whilst Japanese exports fell by 18.4 % to the forecast figure of 980.000 units. Discussions on monitoring levels for 1994 have already begun; these are taking place against a backdrop of stagnation in demand in the EU.

While the Union has committed itself to the gradual opening of the EU market, the Commission will continue to ensure, over the whole transitional period, that the arrangement is applied integrally and in conformity with all its objectives.

At the same time, the Commission welcomes the fact that the move to a better integration of Japanese manufacturing plants into the Union is continuing. In addition there is no evidence of circumvention of the arrangement through exports to the EU of cars from plants in third countries which just assemble kits of parts originating in Japan.

Overall, the Commission believes that the criteria set out under the arrangement remain valid and that the commitment to open the EU market fully by the end of 1999 must be strictly adhered to.

- Market access in the EU

As a result of the Uruguay Round import duties in the EU for cars will be maintained at the present level of 10% whilst the tariff of 11 % on LCV's will be lowered by 1 percentage point only to reach 10%. These results are consistent with the objectives of the arrangement with Japan. EU tariffs on parts or components were reduced by about one third on average as part of the overall package deal. Overall the EU tariff offer in the automotive sector of around 5 % compares to an overall tariff reduction of 37.3 % by the EU.

(ii) Improving Access to Third Markets

With cyclical variations in the major European car markets becoming more pronounced, and the EU economies moving more and more in parallel, it is essential that the EU industry develops a worldwide sales basis which allows production cycles to be smoothed. For this reason comparable and effective market access of EU-produced cars and automotive products to third markets are of the utmost importance to the future development of the industry.

Following the completion of the Uruguay Round negotiations in which a certain if limited progress was made, the Commission, in conjunction with Member States and industry should determine the most important market access barriers to EU exports and draw up a series of market opening objectives and a timetable for achieving them. Particular attention must be paid to the countries where EU car exports are decreasing or remain marginal (USA, Japan and South Korea) and to those countries with considerable growth potential (such as Malaysia, the Philippines and Indonesia) but where local industry continues to be protected through high import duties, local content policies or restrictive licensing systems. As regards China and Taiwan, who are not yet GATT members, the Union will negotiate market access including in the automobile sector, in the context of the negotiations for their GATT membership.

- Major Third Markets Where EU Exports Are Decreasing or Remain Very Limited

- Japan

Under the Trade Assessment Mechanism (TAM), the EU and Japan have agreed to analyse the causes of the relatively low performance on the Japanese markets of those EU products and services which are highly competitive on other markets. In the field of automotive products, the trade of engines and engine parts might offer some development potential, particularly in view of the current high value of the Yen.

Efforts will continue to be devoted to removing the remaining difficulties relating to regulations, technical standards and structural factors (eg zoning regulations). The aim is to reduce the cost of testing of EU cars destined for the Japanese market.

The EU-Japan dialogue on industrial policy and industrial co-operation launched in January 1993 also provides a useful framework for co-operation at industry level. The Commission considers it important to develop actively the participation of EU component manufacturers in design-in programmes and to develop co-operative links between the Japanese industry and EU component and car manufacturers.

The Commission made a formal démarche to the US authorities in 1993 expressing its concern over the risk that the latest round of negotiations between the US and Japan under the "framework agreement" could lead inter alia to discrimination against EU exports of cars and car components to Japan. These negotiations broke down in February when the US attempt to set quantitative targets to measure access to the Japanese car and car parts market was rejected by Japan. The EU has consistently opposed managed trade, market sharing and the use of unilateral trade instruments to achieve trade policy objectives. However, given the market access problem the European industry itself faces in the Japanese market there may now be an opportunity for a trilateral process between the EU, US and Japan to pool ideas with a view to finding a way forward towards opening the Japanese market to more competition in cars, car parts and other sectors.

- USA

EU exports of passenger cars to the United States, which, despite a severe reduction in market share, has remained the most important export market for EU manufacturers, have been handicapped by the triple influence of CAFE, the "gas-guzzler tax" and the luxury tax. Given that EU car producers are strong in the higher market segments, they are particularly affected by the cumulative impact of the taxes. In reality with a market share of less than 4 %, EU producers paid almost 100 % of the CAFE fines, 85 % of the gas guzzler tax and 70 % of the luxury tax. A GATT Panel has been set up to address these issues and will report its findings shortly. The Commission has so far also successfully intervened with the US authorities to prevent tariffs being raised on mini-vans.

- South Korea

The Commission has intervened with the South Korean authorities to demand an opening of the South Korean passenger car market to EU exports. The impact of relatively high tariffs, high internal taxes, including a surtax on cars with a retail price of over 70 million Won (these are only imported cars), and, above all, the government's "frugality campaign" which has turned into a "Buy

Korean campaign", have marginalised import sales in South Korea. In 1992 only 532 EU-produced cars were exported to South Korea (as opposed, for example, to the 40,000 units exported to Taiwan in the same year). It is far from certain that the reduction of South Korean tariffs applied to cars to 15 % in 1993 and to 10 % in 1994 will help to redress the situation. At present, the South Korean car industry is performing strongly; sales of Korean makes on the EU market amounted to about 90,000 in 1993, a market share of about 0.8%. In spite of this, the country still benefits from prefer-ential treatment of its exports to the Union under the Generalised System of Preferences (GSP). Imports of cars from South Korea are subject to a half-yearly zero-duty quota which has been exhausted within days of being opened.

In the new GSP regime for the next ten years, which the Union will elaborate in the light of the conclusions of the Uruguay Round negotiations, the latest developments regarding Korea in particu-lar will be taken into account.

- Third Country Markets with Preferential Access

- EFTA Countries

The bilateral Free Trade Agreements adopted in 1972 and 1973 strengthened economic relations between the EU and the EFTA countries. The EEA Agreement ensures the free circulation of motor vehicles according to the EEC Acquis from 1 January 1994 for most of the technical requirements, and from 1 January 1995 for the environmental requirements. EFTA countries will be, reciprocally, allowed to grant approvals according to Community requirements, and consultations in the decision-making processes will allow future requirements to cover the entire European Economic Area.

The enlargement negotiations with Sweden, Norway, Finland and Austria will lead to the full appli-cation of the EU acquis in these countries in due time, thereby creating fully harmonised conditions in Europe for the further expansion of the industry.

- Central and Eastern European Countries

The Europe Agreements which the EU has signed with Poland, Hungary, the Czech Republic and Slovakia, Bulgaria and Rumania provide inter alia for the establishment of free trade areas and co-operation in the field of standards and conformity assessment.

Pending ratification of the agreements, interim agreements have entered into force in 1992 in the case of Czechoslovakia, and in 1993 in the case of Rumania and Bulgaria. The agreements with Poland and Hungary entered into force in their entirety on 1 February 1994. They provide, in the case of the automotive sector, according to the country or the product, the dismantling of tariff bar-riers over a transitional period. In recognition of the crucial importance that trade plays in the tran-sition of these countries to market economies, the Heads of State and government decided at the European Summit of June 1993, that the Union would dismantle all its tariffs on imports of most industrial products from these countries by 1 January 1995[1] instead of 1 January 1997 as originally provided for in the agreements[2].

The various countries are already giving preferential treatment to certain EU automotive products and will achieve the total dismantling of their barriers by the year 2001 or 2002, pursuant to the agreements. The Commission will ensure that these measures are applied in practice, so that EU manufacturers can take full advantage of such preferences.

---

[1]   1 January 1996 for Romania and Bulgaria.

[2]   EU tariff barriers for the majority of industrial products had been deleted at the time of the entry into force of the agreements.

- <u>Turkey</u>

The Turkish market offers considerable potential, with demand for passenger cars estimated to be increasing by 30 % per annum to reach approximately 800,000 vehicles by 1997. Due to their tariff protection, imports by Turkey remain limited at the moment.

The customs union, foreseen in the Association Agreement of 1964 should be achieved by 1 January 1995. This implies the total dismantling of all Turkish tariff and non-tariff barriers to imports from the Union, and the adoption of the Common Customs Tariff.

Whereas the Union has fulfilled all its obligations in conformity with the Protocol (the total elimination of customs duties), Turkish tariff protection in the automotive sector remains high. From 1 January 1994 important efforts have been made to reduce effective tariffs. This year, customs duties vary from 3 to 6 % and the Mass Housing Fund from 28 to 60 %. Whereas in 1993, there were no preferences for Community vehicles compared to vehicles from third countries, in 1994 preferences ranging from 5 to 7 % are now applicable; in the framework of the EC/Turkey Customs Union discussions, the Commission continues to press Turkey to pursue these efforts.

(5) **Conclusion**

The Commission believes that within the framework of open and competitive markets the contribution of the European Union to the structural adjustment process of the automobile industry aimed at improving its international competitiveness should consist of the following key elements :-

- using Structural policy instruments to facilitate adaptation of enterprises and their workforces to new production systems and to industrial changes;

- taking advantage of joint research and development programmes under the Fourth Framework Programme aimed at undertaking the basic research underpinning future technologies;

- employing renewed efforts to improve the smooth functioning of the internal market;

- removing market access barriers in principal markets and markets with high growth potential worldwide.

It goes without saying, however, that the primary responsibility to effect the changes necessary to improve its competitiveness remains with the industry itself.

COMMUNICATION

on the

EUROPEAN UNION
AUTOMOBILE INDUSTRY

ANNEX

CONTENTS

TABLE 1

New Passenger Car Registrations in the 12 Member States of the EU(1)

(in 1000s)

		% change
1975	7326	-
1976	8350	14.0
1977	8808	5.5
1978	9367	6.4
1979	9554	2.0
1980	9211	-3.6
1981	8950	-2.8
1982	9061	1.3
1983	9496	4.8
1984	9214	-3.0
1985	9554	3.7
1986	10530	10.2
1987	11296	7.3
1988	11876	5.1
1989	12298	3.6
1990	12704	3.3
1991	12549	-1.2
1992	12591	0.3
1993[2]	10666	-15.4

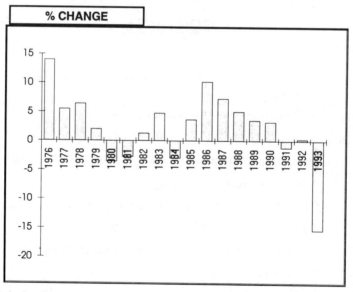

Source: Marketing Systems

---

(1)   Ex-GDR included from 1990 onwards.

(2)   The market declined by 15.9% for cars and LCVs for total 1993.

180

TABLE 2 (a)

<u>EU Trade With Extra-EU: Cars and LCVs</u>
(1000 units)

Year	EU Imports	EU Exports	EU Balance
1985	2235	2315	80
1986	1673	2030	357
1987	1600	1982	382
1988	1623	1872	249
1989	1310	1668	358
1990	1747	1816	69
1991	1945	1556	-389
1992	1903	1576	-327
1992 - (1-6)	1013	803	-210
1993 - (1-6)	758	849	91

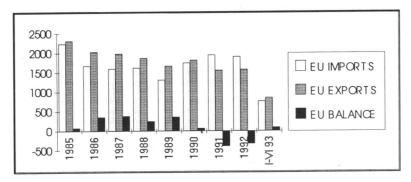

ECU millions

Year	EU Imports	EU Exports	EU Balance
1985	10026	23136	13110
1986	8642	22489	13847
1987	8866	23091	14225
1988	9584	20013	10429
1989	10370	21195	10825
1990	11313	22070	10757
1991	13731	18971	5240
1992	14644	19282	4638
1992 - (1-6)	7749	9527	1778
1993 - (1-6)	6229	10252	4023

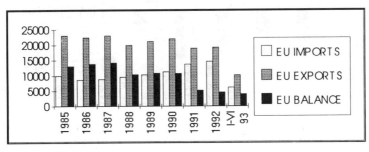

<u>Source</u>: Eurostat - COMEXT

181

TABLE 2 (b)

Trade in New Passenger Cars and LCVs with Japan
(1000 units)

Year	Exports to Japan	Imports from Japan	Net Trade
1989	153	882	-729
1990	183	1232	-1049
1991	134	1374	-1240
1992	104	1198	-1094
1992 - (1-6)	53	646	-593
1993 - (1-6)	52	465	-413

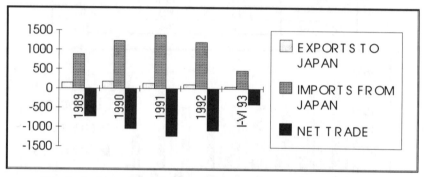

Trade in New Passenger Cars and LCVs with Japan
(ECU millions)

Year	Exports to Japan	Imports from Japan	Net Trade
1989	2555	7505	-4950
1990	3426	7933	-4507
1991	3000	9448	-6448
1992	2233	9563	-7330
1992 - (1-6)	1192	5004	-3812
1993 - (1-6)	991	4051	-3060

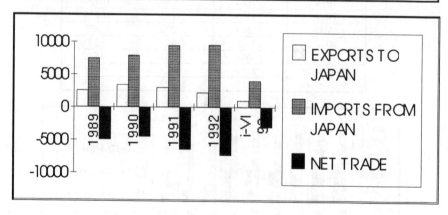

<u>Source</u>: Eurostat - COMEXT

TABLE 3

Production of Passenger Cars in the 12 Member States of the EU[1] (1000s)

		% change
1985	10883	-
1986	11483	5.5
1987	12182	6.1
1988	12723	4.4
1989	13422	5.5
1990	13333	-0.7
1991	12955	-2.8
1992	13230	+2.1
1993[2]	11230	-15.1

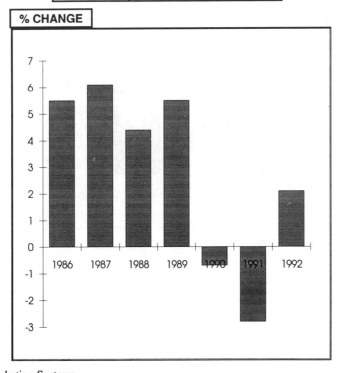

% CHANGE

Source: Marketing Systems

---

[1]   Not adjusted for double counting, which, towards the end of the period under consideration, amounted to circa 550,000 cars per year.

[2]   Estimate.

TABLE 4

Labour Costs in the Car Industry[1] [2]
ECU/hour

Year	European Union	USA	Japan
1980	8.16	9.84	5.25
1985	12.57	25.04	11.33
1990	16.28	16.14	13.35
1991	17.35	17.37	15.74
1992	18.77	16.54	15.86
11/1993	18.91	19.00	21.44

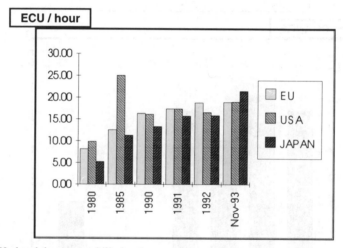

Source: Verband der Automobilindustrie

---

[1]   Including social costs.

[2]   1980-1992: recalculated on the basis of VDA figures.

     11/1993 calculated based on the hypothesis of labour costs in national currencies remaining unchanged on 1992.

TABLE 5

Principal Components of Private Motorization
(Passenger Cars)

Country	Cars per 1000 inhabitants (1992)	New registrations 1992 (1000s)	New registrations Average growth rate 1992-2002 (%)
Belgium	398	466	0.7
Denmark	309	85	5.3
Germany	465	3929	0.3
Greece	166	199	-1.0
Spain	320	979	3.4
France	416	2106	1.4
Ireland	236	68	2.6
Italy	456	2375	0.1
Luxembourg	521	37	2.0
Netherlands	371	492	0.5
Portugal	182	275	2.7
United Kingdom	393	1594	3.8
Western Europe	352	13800	1.5
Eastern Europe	86	1400	9.9
North America	555	8900	1.9
Latin America	63	1500	5.7
Africa	15	300	8.8
Asia	19	7000	3.5
Oceania	455	500	1.8
World	83	34000	2.8

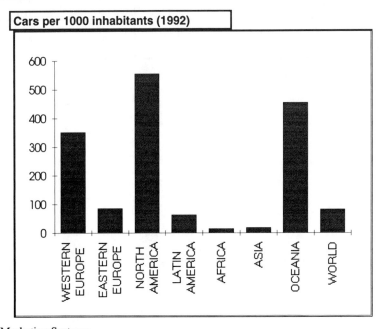

Cars per 1000 inhabitants (1992)

Source: Marketing Systems

TABLE 6

Supply and Demand of Passenger Cars Worldwide (millions)

Regions	Years[1]	1982	1992	2002
Western Europe	NR	10.1	13.8	16.0
	P	10.3	13.7	16.5
	CR	1.02	0.99	1.03
Eastern Europe	NR	1.9	1.4	3.6
	P	2.2	1.8	3.7
	CR	1.16	1.29	1.03
Northern America	NR	8.7	8.9	10.7
	P	5.8	6.7	8.7
	CR	0.67	0.75	0.81
Latin America	NR	1.2	1.5	2.6
	P	1.2	1.9	3.0
	CR	1.0	1.27	1.15
Africa	NR	0.5	0.3	0.7
	P	0.2	0.2	0.4
	CR	0.4	0.67	0.57
Asia	NR	4.1	7.0	9.9
	P	7.2	11.4	13.5
	CR	1.76	1.63	1.36
Oceania	NR	0.5	0.5	0.6
	P	0.3	0.2	0.3
	CR	0.6	0.4	0.5
89 Analysed countries	NR	27.1	33.4	44.1
	P	27.3	35.9	46.1
	CR	1.01	1.07	1.04
Others	NR	0.3	0.6	0.8
	P	0.0	0.0	0.0
World	NR	27.4	34.0	44.9
	P	27.3	35.9	46.1

Source: Marketing Systems.[2]

---

[1] NR = new registrations, P = production, CR = coverage rate (P/NR).

[2] Inconsistencies in international new registration and production statistics mean that NR ≠ P.

TABLE 7

EU Automotive Components Industry
Industry Sizing 1992

Country	Production		Value Added		Employment	
	ECU bn	%	ECU bn	%	1000s	%
Germany	43.6	47	20.9	53	436	46
France	18	19	6.1	15	144	15
UK	10.8	12	4.4	11	150	16
Italy	10.2	11	3.5	9	101	11
Spain	6.9	7	3.1	8	73	8
Rest of EU	3.3	4	2.1	4	36	4
Total	92.7	100	40.1	100	940	100

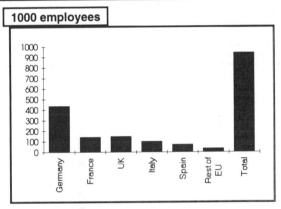

Total Component Demand

Country	ECU bn	%
Germany	39.3	44
France	15.9	18
UK	11.2	13
Italy	9.4	11
Spain	8.2	9
Rest of EU	4.8	5
Total	88.8	100

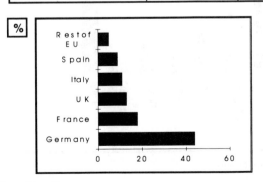

Source: Boston Consulting Group

TABLE 8

EU Automotive Components Industry Consumption (Ecu Bn 1992)

Country	Original Equipment Market		Replacement Equipment Market		Total	
	1992	1999	1992	1999	1992	1999
Germany	34.3	30.5	5.0	5.0	39.4	35.5
France	12.2	13.4	3.8	3.4	15.9	16.8
UK	6.9	13.5	4.3	4.2	11.2	17.7
Italy	6.3	7.6	3.1	3.3	9.4	10.9
Spain	6.5	7.7	1.7	1.8	8.2	9.5
Rest of EU	1.9	3.6	2.8	2.5	4.7	6.1
Total	68.2	76.3	20.6	20.1	88.8	96.4

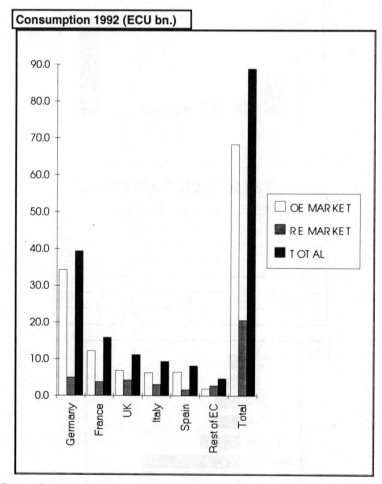

Source: Boston Consulting Group

TABLE 9

Employment In The Motor Vehicles Industry
(Manufacture Of Motor Vehicles And Components - Nace 35)

Year	x1000	index
1980	2213	100.0
1981	2059	93.0
1982	1984	89.7
1983	1940	87.7
1984	1905	86.1
1985	1863	84.2
1986	1832	82.8
1987	1836	83.0
1988	1839	83.1
1989	1855	83.8
1990	1897	85.7
1991	1866	84.3
1992	1821	82.3

Source: Eurostat - COMEXT

Estimates for 1991 and 1992

TABLE 10

Trade in New Passenger Cars and LCVs:
The Union's Most Important Partners in 1992

EXPORTS		
Destination Country	**Units (1000s)**	**Value (ECU millions)**
Austria	245	2453
Switzerland	208	2449
USA	151	3367
Japan	104	2233
Sweden	92	1026

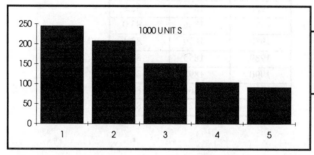

1. AUSTRIA
2. SWITZERLAND
3. USA
4. JAPAN
5. SWEDEN

IMPORTS		
Country of Origin	**Units (1000s)**	**Value (ECU millions)**
Japan	1198	9563
South Korea	87	503
USA	81	1024
Poland	70	195
Sweden	61	965

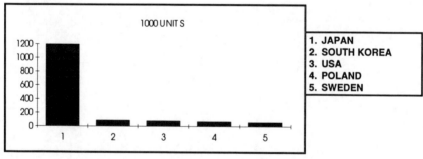

1. JAPAN
2. SOUTH KOREA
3. USA
4. POLAND
5. SWEDEN

Source: Eurostat - COMEXT

TABLE 11

EU Trade in Car Parts and Components:[1]
(ECU millions)

Year	Imports	Exports	Net Trade
1988	4359	6613	2254
1989	4976	6867	1891
1990	4853	6545	1692
1991	5133	7231	2098
1992	5604	7157	1553
1992 - (1-6)	2897	3794	897
1993 - (1-6)	2973	3683	710

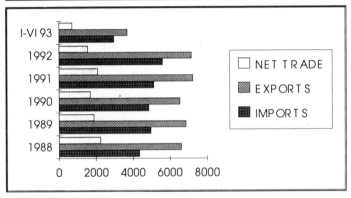

EU Trade in Car Parts and Components:[2]
Most Important Partners in 1992
(ECU millions)

EXPORTS			IMPORTS		
Country of Destination	ECU millions	% Change 1992/1988	Country of Origin	ECU millions	% Change 1992/1988
USA	1090	-38.6	Japan	1379	+25.6
Sweden	772	+3.9	Sweden	1036	+12.7
Austria	554	+53.9	Austria	625	+85.4
Turkey	426	+120.9	USA	573	+31.4
Mexico	397	+218.4	Switzerland	154	+16.3
Japan	261	+92.5	Yugoslavia	82	-25.0
Switzerland	232	+1.0	Brazil	75	+30.4

<u>Source</u>: Eurostat - COMEXT

---

[1]   Including engines and engine parts.

[2]   Excluding engines and engine parts.

6442/94 (Presse 76)

```
┌─────────────────────────────────────────────┐
│                                             │
│          PRESS RELEASE*                     │
│                                             │
│       1750th Council meeting                │
│                                             │
│          - INDUSTRY -                       │
│                                             │
│       Luxembourg, 22 April 1994             │
│                                             │
└─────────────────────────────────────────────┘
```

President :   Mr Konstantinos SIMITIS
                   Minister for Industry of the
                   Hellenic Republic

---

* Only the part of the press release relating to the Council's Resolution on the Automobile Industry is reproduced in this publication.

22.IV.94

The Governments of the Member States and the European Commission were represented as follows:

Belgium:
Mr Robert COLLIGNON   Chairman of the Executive of the Walloon Region

Denmark:
Ms Mimi JAKOBSEN   Minister for Industry and Energy

Germany:
Mr Johann EEKHOFF   State Secretary, Federal Ministry for Economic Affairs

Greece:
Mr Konstantinos SIMITIS   Minister for Industry

Spain:
Mr Juan Manuel EGUIAGARAY   Minister for Industry
Mr Juan Ignacio MOLTO GARCIA   State Secretary for Industry

France:
Mr Pierre de BOISSIEU   Ambassador, Permanent Representative

Ireland:
Mr Ruairi QUINN   Minister for Employment and Enterprise

Italy:
Mr Paolo BARATTA   Minister for Foreign Trade

Luxembourg:
Mr Jean-Jacques KASEL   Ambassador, Permanent Representative

Netherlands:
Mr B.R. BOT   Ambassador, Permanent Representative

Portugal:
Mr Luis MIRA AMARAL   Minister for Industry and Energy
Mr Luis Filipe ALVES MONTEIRO   State Secretary for Industry

United Kingdom:
Mr Tim SAINSBURY   Minister of State, Department of Trade and
                                          Industry

Commission:
Mr Martin BANGEMANN   Member
Mr Karel VAN MIERT   Member
Mr Raniero VANNI D'ARCHIRAFI   Member

AUTOMOBILE INDUSTRY - COUNCIL RESOLUTION

THE COUNCIL OF THE EUROPEAN UNION,

Having regard to the Treaty establishing the European Union,

Having regard to the Commission communication of November 1990 on industrial policy in an open and competitive environment,

Having regard to the Commission's White Paper of December 1993 on growth, competitiveness and employment,

Having regard to the Commission communication from the Commission to the Council and the European Parliament of February 1994 on the European Union automobile industry,

Having regard to the discussions held at the Auto Forum of 1 March 1994, sponsored by the European Commission and the European Parliament,

Whereas the Union's automobile industry - which for this resolution covers both component and vehicle manufacturing - is, and will continue to be, of paramount importance to the Union's economy in terms of employment directly and indirectly depending on it, in terms of its contribution to the economy of the Union and its trade balance, and also in terms of its role in spearheading technological advancement and progress in the organisation of production;

Whereas the automobile industry must continue to adapt its products to meet societal demands for clean, safe, efficient, quality and value cars;

Whereas the automobile industry must make additional efforts to respond to increasing environmental requirements and concerns;

Whereas competition is forcing EU car and component manufacturers to undertake substantial restructuring with the objective of increasing productivity and cost effectiveness along the supply, manufacturing and distribution chain; whereas, in the supply sector, structural adjustment will be particularly important;

Whereas restructuring is taking place against a background of a severe downturn in demand in the Union in 1993;

Whereas it is essential that closer partnership relations between producers and suppliers and between producers and distributors be developed, in order to improve efficiency and competitivity;

Whereas the main responsibility for improving industrial competitiveness lies with all elements of the industry themselves;

Whereas the role of the public authorities is to provide the industry with a clear, stable and predictable framework for their activities and to ensure an environment favourable to competitiveness;

Whereas the Union's approach to industrial policy centres on the completion of the single market, the application of the competition rules, the use of horizontal policy instruments in the field of research and development and structural funds and on assuring equal access to markets and fair competition on a global scale;

Whereas strong efforts in the field of research and development, particularly in the areas of both product, process and production technology, are vital for the future competitive position of this industry;

Whereas the structural adjustment of the automobile industry, which presents different characteristics in the Member States, has important regional and social effects;

Whereas the necessary introduction of new technologies within the automobile sector depends crucially on the availability of people with the relevant skills and whereas that might entail reconversion of parts of the labour force on all levels;

Whereas it is essential for the European Union automobile industry to have better access to third country markets;

CONFIRMING THE CONCLUSIONS OF ITS RESOLUTION OF 17 June 1992 ([1]), THE COUNCIL HEREBY ADOPTS THIS RESOLUTION :

- I -

THE COUNCIL:

1. recognizes that the Union has an important role to play in creating a favourable business environment for the automobile industry which sets an appropriate framework for a future-oriented and coherent approach to the development, production, distribution and use of the automobile and its impact on the environment and on society as a whole;

2. underlines that the structural adjustment of the industry and measures to facilitate such adjustment are a matter of urgency, in order to prepare the full opening of the EU market to Japanese competition in the year 2000 and in light of the emergence of new strong competitors from other countries;

3. recognises that to be successful, structural adjustment must take place in a stable and predictable regulatory policy environment, which takes account of the cost-effectiveness of regulatory measures, including their impact on the automobile industry's overall competitiveness, whilst giving industry sufficient lead time to adapt to necessary regulatory changes;

([1]) OJ No C 178, 15.7.92, p. 6.

4. underlines the growing importance of component manufacturing and the further development of the outsourcing of systems and component production to suppliers within the automobile manufacturing value added chain, which is essential to increase the competitiveness of the automobile sector as a whole;

5. recognises that, where appropriate for the proper functioning of the single market, consideration should be given to further harmonisation of relevant legislation concerning the automobile sector;

6. emphasises that the environmental problems related to the use of automobiles

    -   emissions, noise, congestion and solid waste from the scrapping of used vehicles - must be progressively and significantly reduced; in this context, the Council welcomes the adoption of the directive leading to a further reduction of car emissions from 1996 for new vehicle types;

7. emphasizes that the Commission should reach a decision quickly on how Regulation No 123/85 on Selective and Exclusive Distribution in the automobile industry should be applied in the future, taking account of the specific nature of and competition in the sector, the functioning of the existing Regulation, progress in the internal market, the need to reinforce partnership relations between different elements of the distribution chain, in order to improve industrial efficiency and competitiveness, the balance of interests between the parties concerned (constructors, parts producers, distributors, consumers) and the contribution that the Regulation makes to the efficient management of the arrangement between Japan and the EU on trade in automobiles which should not be weakened in any way;

8. emphasises that public policy in the field of R&TD must be optimised through effective co-ordination of Union, national and EUREKA programmes and projects; with regard to Community programmes under the Fourth Framework Programme, a strengthened dialogue with appropriate industrial panels and better co-ordination and consultation between individual research programmes should be achieved in order to achieve the best long-term return on R&TD investment in terms of sustained industrial competitiveness throughout the industry;

9. emphasises the need to enhance efforts relating to the provision of training at all levels in order to:

    -   anticipate the effects of restructuring on employment; in this context training programmes based on the introduction of new production methods and to encourage SMEs to adapt to new forms of co-operation with major companies are of particular relevance,

    -   make changes economically efficient and socially acceptable,

    -   help in retraining and redeployment,

    -   promote best practice within the industry;

Community horizontal instruments can support the industry's own efforts, notably through Structural Funds, while complying with the powers that the Regulations on the Structural Funds confer on the Member States, in particular in the framework of industrial mutations, and through the use of appropriate Community Initiative programmes;

10. emphasises that, in order to support the Community's policy of international trade and competition, it is necessary to eliminate barriers preventing the European automobile industry from penetrating high-growth third markets, including barriers in the field of technical regulations, distribution, competition policy and foreign investment;

11. takes the view that, for the necessary changes to materialise, and for the European industry to become more flexible and more competitive, dialogue between the social partners should take place based on mutual trust, at the appropriate level, and according to national practices.

- II -

THE COUNCIL INVITES THE COMMISSION:

Within the horizontal industrial policy framework adopted by the Union, the Commission should facilitate the structural adjustment process of the industry which is vital to its improved competitiveness and thereby to its future. In particular, the Council calls on the Commission:

1. to co-ordinate and organize its programmes in the field of R&TD in such a way as to cover themes relevant to improved competitiveness, to facilitate access to the programmes for component suppliers notably SMEs as well as their participation in consortia with vehicle manufacturers, to improve the dissemination of research results, and to facilitate industry planning in this sphere by presenting a clear view on the possibilities of funding projects covering several programme activities; in this context, the dialogue with industry should be further developed;

2. to encourage industrial co-operation by SMEs in the components sector both among themselves and with the vehicle manufacturers in order to bolster improved and faster exploitation of R&D results to obtain new products and in order to strengthen improvements in production procedures and the organization of work, areas in which the European industry lags behind its competitors;

3. to reach a decision quickly, following full and proper consultations with all interested parties, on how Commission Regulation No 123/85 on selective and exclusive distribution should be applied in the future taking account of all elements referred to above;

4. to continue to promote better environmental and safety performance of auto-mobiles by developing advanced environmental and technical standards which, within the context of global and multifaceted approaches to these problems, are cost-effective and achievable in a realistic time schedule in the overall context of a stable and predictable regulatory policy environment; in drawing up such measures, account should be taken of their impact on the industry's overall competitiveness;

5. to develop and to propose coherent policies, e.g. in the environmental and infra-structural sphere, impacting the future context of car use and which are thus of crucial importance to the car industry;

6. to continue to apply integrally and in conformity with all its objectives, the arrangement on automobiles with Japan which provides for the progressive opening of the EU market over a transitional period ending on 31 December 1999;

7. to draw up a list of the most important barriers impeding better market access for EU automobiles on third markets; on the basis of this list a market opening plan should be drawn up together with a timetable for achieving results; progress should be reported to the Council under Article 113 of the Treaty;

8. to promote industrial co-operation and business contacts in the automobile sector with third countries, notably Japan, in areas where the greatest value added can be achieved at Union level;

9. to report to the Council and the European Parliament by the end of 1995 on the progress achieved in implementing this Resolution and on the industry's struc-tural adjustment. An interim report should be made to the Directors-General of Industry.

- III -

THE COUNCIL CALLS ON THE MEMBER STATES AND THE COMMISSION to actively pursue the aforementioned objectives, in accordance with their respective powers.

EUROPEAN PARLIAMENT - EUROPEAN COMMISSION

FORUM ON THE EUROPEAN AUTOMOBILE INDUSTRY

LIST OF PARTICIPANTS

BRUSSELS, 1 MARCH 1994

Mr J. Adams
TRANSPORT AND GENERAL WORKERS' UNION
Smith Square
GB-SW1 LONDON
UNITED KINGDOM

Mr L. Asencio Portilla
FEDERACIÓN DEL METAL CC. OO.
Miembro de Comité de Empresa Ford
Fernandez de la Hoz 12, 2°
E - 28010 MADRID
ESPAÑA

Mr J. Antila
METTALLITYÖVÄEN LIITTO R.Y. (METALLI)
Economist
Siltasaarenkatu 3-5A, P.O. Box 107 116
SF-00531 HELSINKI 53
SUOMI/FINLAND

Mr N. Atkins
BARKING & DAGENHAM POST
Economic Correspondent
2, Whalebone Lane South
GB-RM8 1HB DAGENHAM
UNITED KINGDOM

Mr A. Antonelli
ITALIAN PERMANENT REPRESENTATION TO THE
EUROPEAN UNION
Industrial Attaché
9, rue du Marteau
B-1040 BRUXELLES
BELGIEN/BELGIQUE/BELGIË

Mr P. Aubin
ERAFA
President
Belchenstr. 64
D-76532 BADEN-BADEN
DEUTSCHLAND

Ms G. Arehorn
SWEDISH UNION OF CLERICAL AND TECHNICAL
EMPLOYEES IN INDUSTRY
Trade Union Official
Olof Palmes gata 11
S-105 32 STOCKHOLM
SVERIGE

Mr P. Axell
BORGSTENA TEXTILE Ltd
Manager Director
Box 74
S-513 02 BORGSTENA
SVERIGE

Mr M. Aribart
MINISTERE DE L'INDUSTRIE, DES POSTES ET
TELECOMMUNICATIONS ET DU C.E.
Chargé de Mission
3-5 rue Barbet de Joug
F-75353 PARIS 07 SP
FRANCE

Mr J. Balthazar
PAYS DE FRANCHE-COMTÉ
Journaliste
21, place Denfert-Rochereau
F-25200 MONTBELIARD
FRANCE

Mr C. Bourgoignie
START 2000 S.A.
6 champs du Vert Chasseur
B-1180 BRUXELLES
BELGIEN/BELGIQUE/BELGIË

Mr D. Buda
EUROPEAN COMMISSION
DG V - Emploi, relations industrielles et affaires sociales
Rue de la Loi, 200
B-1049 BRUXELLES
BELGIEN/BELGIQUE/BELGIË

Mr J. Bowman
WEST MIDLANDS ENTERPRISE BOARD Ltd
Senior Consultant
31-34 Waterloo Street
GB-B2 5TJ BIRMINGHAM
UNITED KINGDOM

Dr R. Buescher
EUROPEAN COMMISSION
Member of Mr Bangemann's Cabinet
Rue de la Loi, 200
B-1049 BRUXELLES
BELGIEN/BELGIQUE/BELGIË

Mr P. Broos
MORET ERNST & YOUNG
Senior Consultant
P.O. Box 2295
NL-3000 C.G. ROTTERDAM
NEDERLAND

Mr F. Buggenhoudt
VOLKSWAGEN BRUSSEL
Syndikaal Afgewaardigde BBTK-SETCA
Tweede Britse Le Gerlaan, 201
B-1190 BRUXELLES
BELGIEN/BELGIQUE/BELGIË

Ms C. Bruetschy
EUROPEAN COMMISSION
C/o RP6 - 3/30 (M. WRIGHT)
Rue de la Loi, 200
B-1049 BRUXELLES
BELGIEN/BELGIQUE/BELGIË

Mr Burden
HOUSE OF COMMONS
Member of Parliament
Westminster
GB-SW1A 8AA LONDON
UNITED KINGDOM

Mr H. Bruls
AGENCE EUROPE
Bld St Lazare
B-1210 BRUXELLES
BELGIEN/BELGIQUE/BELGIË

Mr T. Burns
LANCASHIRE COUNTY COUCIL
County Councillor
P.O. BOX 78
GB-PRI 8XJ PRESTON
UNITED KINGDOM

Mr B. Byrne
SERVICES INDUSTRIAL, PROFESSIONAL AND TECHNICAL
UNION
Electronics and Engineering branch
Liberty Hall
IRL- DUBLIN 1
IRELAND

Ms S. Camusso
FLM FIOM-CGIL (UILM)
Secretary, Automobile Industry
Corse Trieste, 36
I-00198 ROMA
ITALIA

Mr J. Byrne
TRANSPORT AND GENERAL WORKERS' UNION
Lucas Industres (Executive)
28, Chetwynd Road, War End
GB-B8 2LA BIRMINGHAM
UNITED KINGDOM

Mr J. Candries
FORD OF EUROPE INCORPORATED
Directeur
Affaires Européennes
2, Boulevard de la Woluwé, Bte 4
B-1150 BRUXELLES
BELGIEN/BELGIQUE/BELGIË

Mr Cagnard
RENAULT S.A.
Relations extérieures
Quai du Point du Jour, 34
F-92109 BOULOGNE-BILLANCOURT
FRANCE

Mr N.A. Carlsson
SVENSKA METALL
Research Department
Olof Palmes Gata 11
S-105 52 STOCKHOLM
SVERIGE

Mr M.J. Callaghan
FORD OF EUROPE
Central Office Eagle Way Brentwood
GB-CM13 3BW ESSEX
UNITED KINGDOM

Ms R. Carré
NISSAN EUROPE N.V.
Assistant
avenue Louise 287 - Bte 4
B - 1050 BRUSSELS
BELGIEN/BELGIQUE/BELGIË

Mr C. Camerana
MAGNETI MARELLI S.p.a.
Deputy Chairman of the Board
Viale Aldo Borletti 61
I-20011 CORBETTA
ITALIA

Mr G. Cartwright
BBA GROUP PLC
Chief executief
Friction Materials Division
P.O. BOX 18
GB-BD19 3UJ CLECKHEATON-WEST
UNITED KINGDOM

Mr H. Dalibor
VOLKSWAGEN AG
Manager
Godesberger allee 90
D-53175 BONN
DEUTSCHLAND

Mr P. Day
BBC RADIO
GB-W1 1AA LONDON
UNITED KINGDOM

Mr G. Dancet
COMMISSION EUROPEENNE
C150-6/104
Rue de la Loi 200
B-1049 BRUXELLES
BELGIEN/BELGIQUE/BELGIË

Ms B. De Castelmau
CCFA
Responsable Département Economie Statistiques
2, rue de Presbourg
F-75008 PARIS
FRANCE

Doctor B. Dankbaar
MAASTRICHT ECONOMIC RESEARCH INSTITUTE ON
INNOVATION AND TECHNOLOGY
Programme Leader
Tongerestraat 49, P.O. Box 1616
NL-6200 MD MAASTRICHT
NEDERLAND

Mr J. De Juan Saez
REPRESENTATION PERMANENTE DE L'ESPAGNE
AUPRES DE L'UNION EUROPEENNE
Bd. du Régent 52
B-1000 BRUXELLES
BELGIEN/BELGIQUE/BELGIË

Mr Á. Danyi
HUNGARIAN METALWORKER' UNION
International Secretary
Magdolna u. 5-7
H-1086 BUDAPEST
MAGYARORSZAG

Mr F. De Mulder
GENERAL MOTORS CONTINENTAL
Purchasing Executive
Noorderlaan 75
B-2030 ANTWERP
BELGIEN/BELGIQUE/BELGIË

Mr L.S. Davies
ROVER GROUP plc
Bickenhill Lane, Bickenhill
GB-B37 7HQ BIRMINGHAM
UNITED KINGDOM

Mr E. De Schrijver
GENERAL MOTORS COORDINATION CENTER
President automotive trade group of Fabrimetal
Neerveldstraat 107
B-1200 BRUSSEL
BELGIEN/BELGIQUE/BELGIË

Mr K. Done
FINANCIAL TIMES
GB-SE1 9HL LONDON
UNITED KINGDOM

Dr A. Enrietti
DIPARTIMENTO DI ECONOMIA - UNIVERISTÀ DI TORINO
Researcher
Via Po 53
I-10124 TURIN
ITALIA

Dr I. Drymoussis
REPRESENTATION PERMANENTE DE LA GRECE AUPRES
DE L'UNION EUROPEENNE
Head of Division on Economic & Financial Affairs
Av. de Cortenberg 71
B-1040 BRUXELLES
BELGIEN/BELGIQUE/BELGIË

Ms S. Ernst
PORSCHE AG
Referee of the works council
Porschestrasse 42
D-70435 STUTTGART-ZUFFENHAUSEN
DEUTSCHLAND

Mr E. Dufeil
EUROPEAN COMMISSION
DG XVI, Regional Policy
Rue de la Loi, 200
B-1049 BRUXELLES
BELGIEN/BELGIQUE/BELGIË

Ms B. Ernst de la Graete
EUROPEAN PARLIAMENT
Member of Parliament
rue Belliard 97-113
B-1047 BRUXELLES
BELGIEN/BELGIQUE/BELGIË

Mr K. Ellegast
PHOENIX A.G.
Hannoverstrasse 88, P.O. Box 900854
D-21048 HAMBURG
DEUTSCHLAND

Mr A. Escudero
CLEPA
Castelló 120
E-28006 MADRID
ESPAÑA

Ms E. Eller-Braatz
IG-METALL-VORSTANDSVERWALTUNG
Abt. Wirtschaft
Lyonerstrasse 32
D-60519 FRANKFURT/MAIN
DEUTSCHLAND

Mr D.J. Evans
RETAIL MOTOR INDUSTRY FEDERATION Ltd.
Legal and International Affairs Director
201, Great Portland Street
GB-W1N 6AB LONDON
UNITED KINGDOM

Mr N. Fridhi
AL HAYAT
Journaliste
15, rue Philippe le Bon
B-1040 BRUXELLES
BELGIEN/BELGIQUE/BELGIË

Mr G. Garuzzo
ASSOCIATION DES CONSTRUCTEURS EUROPEENS
D'AUTOMOBILES (ACEA)
President of the ACEA
211, rue du Noyer
B-1040 BRUXELLES
BELGIEN/BELGIQUE/BELGIË

Mr A. Furia
FIEV
rue J. J. Rousseau 77-81
F-92158 SURESNES
FRANCE

Mr W. Gersen
INDUSTRIEBOND FNV
Postbus 5430
NL-6130 PK SITTARD
NEDERLAND

Mr M. Gallardo
FEDERACIÓN SIDEROMETALURGICA
avda. de América 25,5°
E-28008 MADRID
ESPAÑA

Dr S. Ghezzi
J.M. DIDIER & ASSOCIATES
Consultant
Rue Vergote 11
B-1040 BRUXELLES
BELGIEN/BELGIQUE/BELGIË

Ms G. Galloy
UNION DES INDUSTRIES FERROVIAIRES EUROPEENNES
Economist Assistant to the Secretary General
Rue de Stassart, 93
B-1050 BRUXELLES
BELGIEN/BELGIQUE/BELGIË

Mr M. Gidlow
FORD OF BRITAIN
Manager Power Train Product Development
Research and Engineering Centre
Laindon Basildon
GB-SS15 6EE ESSEX
UNITED KINGDOM

Ms O. Garnier
CNPA
50, rue Rouget de Lisle
F-92158 SURESNES
FRANCE

Mr A. Goffaux
VOLKSWAGEN BRUXELLES
Délégué CNE
201, Boulevard de la 2ième Armée Britannique
B-1190 BRUXELLES
BELGIEN/BELGIQUE/BELGIË

Mr R. Guasco
CLEPA/FIEV
Technical Secretary/Deputy Executive Director
79 rue J.J. Rousseau
F-92158 SURESNES CEDEX
FRANCE

Mr M.J-C. Harbour
HARBOUR WADE AUTOMOTIVE CONSULTANCY
Managing Partner
Manour Road
GB-B91 2BL SOLIHULL
UNITED KINGDOM

Mr J.L. Guichard
Syndicat CFDT de la Métallurgie de Sochaux-Montbéliard
Secrétaire Général du syndicat CFDT de la Métallurgie
41, rue Louis Renard
70 400 HERICOURT
FRANCE

Mr S. Hart
TRANSPORT & GENERAL WORKERS UNION DAGENH
(FORD)
District Officer
76, Rainham road
GB-RM13 7RE RAINHAM ESSEX
UNITED KINGDOM

Mr G. Guillonneau
RENAULT VOLVO REPRESENTATION TO THE EC
Permanent Representative
Av. de la Joyeuse Entrée 14 / 6
B-1040 BRUSSELS
BELGIEN/BELGIQUE/BELGIË

Dr P. Hartz
MITGLIED DES VORSTANDES DER VOLKSWAGEN AG
Berliner Ring 2
D-38440 WOLFSBURG
DEUTSCHLAND

Mr F. Haberl
MAHAG
Vice Président of the CECRA
Schleibingerstrasse 12
D-8000 MÜNCHEN
DEUTSCHLAND

Dr P. Hasselberg
BUNDESMINISTERIUM FÜR WIRTSCHAFT
D-53107 BONN
DEUTSCHLAND

Mr A. Ham
BOSAL INTERNATIONAL S.A.
c/o RAI Vereniging, P.O. Box 74800
NL-1070 DM AMSTERDAM
NEDERLAND

Mr J.C. Hawksby
BEDFORDSHIRE COUNTY COUNCIL
Chairman
19 Bedford road
GB-MK43 OEW CRANFIELD - BEDFORDSHIRE
UNITED KINGDOM

Mr I. Högfeldt
ARVIKA GJUTERI AB
Managing Director
Korpralsvagen 5
S-67182 ARVIKA
SVERIGE

Mr J.M. Hugard
CONFEDERATION FRANCAISE DES TRAVAILLEURS
CHRETIENS
Représentant Syndical Automobiles
3, rue de Hartmannswiller
F-68700 WATTWILLER
FRANCE

Mr C. Hogguer
CENTRALE NATIONALE DES EMPLOYES
Délégué Syndical C.N.E.
Rue Fr. Verdonck 10, bte 84
B-1140 BRUXELLES
BELGIEN/BELGIQUE/BELGIË

Mr M. Hugen
EUROPEAN COMMISSION
DG III E/2 - 4/71 (MICROELECTRONICS)
Rue de la Loi, 200
B-1049 BRUXELLES
BELGIEN/BELGIQUE/BELGIË

Mr M.L. Hollingsworth
SOCIETY OF MOTOR MANUFACTURERS AND TRADERS
Chief Economist
Halkin street
GB-SWIX 7DS LONDON
UNITED KINGDOM

Mr T. Hurst
CITY OF SUNDERLAND
Principal Economic Development Officer
Chief Executives' Department
P.O.Box 100, Civic Centre
GB-SR2 7DN SUNDERLAND
UNITED KINGDOM

Mr L. Holmqvist
SV. EMISSIONSTEKNIK AB
V. Hasselblads G. 8
S-412 31 GÖTEBORG
SVERIGE

Mr S. Ino
DAIHATSU MOTOR Co. Ltd
General Manager
Hermesstraat 8c
B-1930 ZAVENTEM
BELGIEN/BELGIQUE/BELGIË

Mr K. Hubery-Allen
COVENTRY CITY COUNCIL
City Development Directorate
Much Park Street, Tower Book
GB-CV1 2PY COVENTRY
UNITED KINGDOM

Dr A. Insola
STUDIO LEADER EUROPA
Consultant
Square Marguerite 14, Bte 32
B-1040 BRUXELLES
BELGIEN/BELGIQUE/BELGIË

Ms A. Kahn
LE MONDE
rue Falguière 15
F-75015 PARIS
FRANCE

Mr F. Karamitsos
EUROPEAN COMMISSION
Bu 29 - 2/20
Rue de la Loi, 200
B-1049 BRUXELLES
BELGIEN/BELGIQUE/BELGIË

Dr M. Kalk
CLEPA
Secretary-General
rue de Stassart 93
B - 1050 BRUXELLES
BELGIEN/BELGIQUE/BELGIË

Ms E. Karlsson
EFTA SURVEILLANCE AUTHORITY
Officer
Rue Marie-Thérèse 1-3
B-1040 BRUXELLES
BELGIEN/BELGIQUE/BELGIË

Mr F. Kapner
BLOOMBERG BUSINESS NEWS
Journaliste
8 Ave Kleber
F-75116 PARIS
FRANCE

Ms D. Kars
RAI VERENIGING
Postbus 74800
NL-1070 DM AMSTERDAM
NEDERLAND

Mr J. Kapstein
ARCO CHEMICAL PRODUCTS EUROPE
Director, Government Relations
rue de Trèves 45
B-1040 BRUXELLES
BELGIEN/BELGIQUE/BELGIË

Mr R. King
SOCIETY OF MOTOR MANUFACTURERS AND TRADERS
Director of External Affairs
Halkin street
GB-SWIX 7DS LONDON
UNITED KINGDOM

Mr G. Kara
ECOLE PRATIQUE DES HAUTES ETUDES COMMERCIALES
Cortil des Grillon 16
B-1348 LOUVAIN-LA-NEUVE
BELGIEN/BELGIQUE/BELGIË

Mr J.P. Kirschen
FIAT S.p.A.
Vice-Président
Fiat Delegation to Europe
Rue du Luxembourg, 16b
B-1040 BRUXELLES
BELGIEN/BELGIQUE/BELGIË

Mr E. Landaburu
COMMISSION EUROPEENNE
Director General, DG XVI
DGXVI-Regional Policy
Rue de la Loi, 200
B-1049 BRUXELLES
BELGIEN/BELGIQUE/BELGIË

Mr J.C. Lefebvre
RADIO FRANCE BELFORT
Centre des quatre as
F-90 000 BELFORT
FRANCE

Mr C. Lanners
MINISTERE DE L'ECONOMIE
Inspecteur principal
Service de l'Industrie
19-21 Boulevard Royal
L-2914 LUXEMBOURG
LUXEMBOURG

Mr A. Lehmann
CHARLES RILEY CONSULTANTS INTERNATIONAL
Directeur Associé
35, rue Fortuny
F-75017 PARIS
FRANCE

Mr S. Larrañeta Goldaraz
FEDERATION UGT-METAL ZARAGOZA
c/. Costa 1
E-50001 ZARAGOZA
ESPAÑA

Mr K. Lehmann
WIRTSCHAFTSVERBAND STAHLVERFORMUNG
Leiter der Europaabteilung
Goldene Pforte 1
D-58093 HAGEN
DEUTSCHLAND

Mr R.J. Lawrie
THE SOCIETY OF MOTOR MANUFACTURERS AND
TRADERS Ltd
Head of Quality Improvement
Forbes House, Halkin Street
GB-SW1X 7DS LONDON
UNITED KINGDOM

Mr P. Lenoir
VOLVO EUROPA TRUCK
Hoofdafgevaardigde
Noordenbos 3
B-9270 LAARNE
BELGIEN/BELGIQUE/BELGIË

Mr J. Lawson
DRI/McGRAW-HILL
Director of Research
1, Hartfield Road
GB-SW19 3R4 LONDON
UNITED KINGDOM

Mr H. Lense
MERCEDES BENZ AG
Betriebsratvorsitzender
Wekr Untertürkheim, HPC E 606
D-70322 STUTTGART
DEUTSCHLAND

Eng. E. Lopes Rodrigues
DIRECCÃO GERAL DA INDÚSTRIA
Av. Cons. Fernando de Sousa, 11
P-1000 LISBOA
PORTUGAL

Mr W.G. Luding
EUROPEAN PETROLEUM INDUSTRY ASSOCIATION
Deputy Secretary General
Madou Plaza, Place Madou 1
B-1030 BRUXELLES
BELGIEN/BELGIQUE/BELGIË

Mr R.S. Lopez Rodriguez
RED ESPAÑOLA DE CIUDADES DEL AUTOMOVIL
Secretario
c/ Ramon y Cajal
E - 47005 VALLADOLID
ESPAÑA

Mr K. Ludvigsen
LUDVIGSEN ASSOCIATES LIMITED
Chairman
73, Collier Street
GB-NI7JU LONDON
UNITED KINGDOM

Mr J. Lopez-Sanchez
EUROPEAN COMMISSION
DG I - External Relations
Rue de la Loi, 200
B-1049 BRUXELLES
BELGIEN/BELGIQUE/BELGIË

Mr J. Luostarinen
EFTA SURVEILLANCE AUTHORITY
Rue Marie-Thérèse 1-3
B-1040 BRUXELLES
BELGIEN/BELGIQUE/BELGIË

Mr N. Louvet
MINISTERE DES AFFAIRES ECONOMIQUES BELGES
Directeur Général de l'Industrie
Sq. de Meêus 23
B-1040 BRUXELLES
BELGIEN/BELGIQUE/BELGIË

Prof.Dr H.O. Luthe
CATHOLIC UNIVERSITY OF EICHSTÄTT
Professor of Sociology
Ostenstrasse 26
D-385071 EICHSTÄTT
DEUTSCHLAND

Ms M. Luciani
AUTO OGGI
Journalist
I-20090 SEGRATE (MILANO)
ITALIA

Mr H. Mac Dermot
COMMISSION EUROPEENNE
Rue de la Loi 200
B-1049 BRUXELLES
BELGIEN/BELGIQUE/BELGIË

Mr D. McConnell
THE SOCIETY OF MOTOR MANUFACTURERS AND TRADE
Government Affairs Officer
Forbes House, Halkin Street
GB-SW1X 7DS LONDON
UNITED KINGDOM

Mr T. Mogensen
A/S/ROULUNDS FABRIKER
Vice-President
Hestehaven
DK-5260 ODENSE S
DANMARK

Mr N. McGreevy
TRANSPORT & GENERAL WORKERS UNION DAGENHAM
(FORD)
Rover Cars Convenor
21, Saville Close, Rednal
GB-B45 8EN BIRMINGHAM
UNITED KINGDOM

Mr H. Mohl
ROBERT BOSH Gmbh
Vice President
International Sales Coordination Automotive Equipment
Postfach 10 60 50
D-7000 STUTTGART
DEUTSCHLAND

Mr J. McHendry
PEUGEOT TALBOT UK Ltd
Convenor T.G.W.U.
5, Esterton Close, Holbrooks
GB-CV6 4EZ COVENTRY
UNITED KINGDOM

Ms P. Mollet
ASSOCIATION DES CONSTRUCTEURS EUROPEENS
D'AUTOMOBILES (ACEA)
211, rue du Noyer
B-1040 BRUXELLES
BELGIEN/BELGIQUE/BELGIË

Mr L. Merel
FO METAUX
Délégué Syndical Central
Rue Baudoin, 9
F-75013 PARIS
FRANCE

Mr E. Montoya
FEDERACIÓN SIDEROMETALURGICA
avda. de América 25,5°
E-28008 MADRID
ESPAÑA

Mr K.H. Mihr
EUROPEAN PARLIAMENT
Membre du Parlement Européen
Schwerinerweg 4
D-3505 GUDENSBERG
DEUTSCHLAND

Dr K. Morgan
UNIVERSITY OF WALES COLLEGE OF CARDIFF
Faculty of Engineering & Environmental Design
P.O. Box 68
GB-CF1 3XA CARDIFF
UNITED KINGDOM

Mr T. Osawa
NISSAN EUROPE N.V.
Manager
avenue Louise 287 - Bte 4
B - 1050 BRUSSELS
BELGIEN/BELGIQUE/BELGIË

Ms M. Paemen
ASSOCIATION DES CONSTRUCTEURS EUROPEENS
D'AUTOMOBILES (ACEA)
rue du Noyer 211
B-1040 BRUXELLES
BELGIEN/BELGIQUE/BELGIË

Mr H. Oschwendtner
ROBERT BOSCH GmbH
K8/BGE - G
Tübinger Str. 123
D-7410 REUTLINGEN
DEUTSCHLAND

Mr L. Paesschierssens
MINISTERE DES AFFAIRES ECONOMIQUES BELGES
Conseiller Adjoint
Sq. de Meêus 23
B-1040 BRUXELLES
BELGIEN/BELGIQUE/BELGIË

Mr J.M. Otaegi
FTM-ELAMETAL
Apartado de Correos 1.391
E-48009 BILBAO
ESPAÑA

Mr A. Paolicchi
COMMISSION EUROPEENNE
DGI-Relations Economiques Extérieures
Rue de la Loi, 200
B-1049 BRUXELLES
BELGIEN/BELGIQUE/BELGIË

Mr B. Ovesson
MEFAB
Managing Director
Box 152
S-385 00 TORSÅS
SVERIGE

Mr A. Paouicchi
EUROPEAN COMMISSION
DG I
Bld Brand Whitlock 8, Bte 34
B-1150 BRUXELLES
BELGIEN/BELGIQUE/BELGIË

Mr Paelinck
COMMISSION EUROPEENNE
AN80 - 4/24
Rue de la Loi 200
B-1049 BRUXELLES
BELGIEN/BELGIQUE/BELGIË

Mr R. Patten
IGA EUROPE
Public Affairs Consultant
Avenue de Tervuren 55
B-1040 BRUXELLES
BELGIEN/BELGIQUE/BELGIË

Mr F. Poulematis
FR3 TV
chaussée de Louvain 550
B-1030 BRUXELLES
BELGIEN/BELGIQUE/BELGIË

Ms C. Randrio-Move
PARLEMENT EUROPEEN
Membre du Parlement Européen
Rue Belliard 97-113
B-1047 BRUXELLES
BELGIEN/BELGIQUE/BELGIË

Mr J. Puchades Aguilar
FEDERACIÓN PAIS VALENCIA UGT-METAL
c/. Arquitecto MORA 7, 4°
E-46010 VALENCIA
ESPAÑA

Eng. L. Redolfi
VALEO S.p.A.
National Director
Via Asti 89
I-10026 SANTENA
ITALIA

Mr J. Puig
COMMISSION EUROPEENNE
DG XXI - MDB 5/22 A
Rue de la Loi 200
B-1049 BRUXELLES
BELGIEN/BELGIQUE/BELGIË

Mr C. Rey Del Castillo
REPRESENTATION PERMANENTE DE L'ESPAGNE
AUPRES DE L'UNION EUROPEENNE
Bd. du Régent 52
B-1000 BRUXELLES
BELGIEN/BELGIQUE/BELGIË

Dr M. Raisch
DAIMLER-BENZ AG, KONZERNREPRASENTANZ BRÜSSEL
General Manager
133, rue Froissart
B-1040 BRUSSELS
BELGIEN/BELGIQUE/BELGIË

Mr J.P. Reynier
ASSOCIATION DES CONSTRUCTEURS EUROPEENS
D'AUTOMOBILES (ACEA)
Secretary General
211, rue du Noyer
B-1040 BRUXELLES
BELGIEN/BELGIQUE/BELGIË

Mr J. Ramer
DE VOLKSKRANT
Postbus 1000
NL-1000 BA AMSTERDAM
NEDERLAND

Mr A. Richemond
Consultant Economist
26, rue de la Pépinière
F-75008 PARIS
FRANCE

Prof. G. Sacco
UNIVERSITÀ LUISS
Facoltà di Economia
Viale Pola 12
I-00198 ROMA
ITALIA

Ms G. Schaal
DAIMLER-BENZ CORPORATE REPRESENTATION
rue Froissart 133 /29
B-1040 BRUSSELS
BELGIEN/BELGIQUE/BELGIË

Mr A. Sainjon
EUROPEAN PARLIAMENT
97-113 rue Belliard
B-1047 BRUSSELS
BELGIEN/BELGIQUE/BELGIË

Dr A. Schaub
COMMISSION EUROPEENNE
Deputy Director General for Industry
DGIII-Industry
Rue de la Loi, 200
B-1049 BRUXELLES
BELGIEN/BELGIQUE/BELGIË

Ms D. Sakarova
ODBOROVY SVAZ KOVO
International Secretary
Namesti W. Churchilla 2
CZ-11359 PRAHA 3
CESKO REPUBLIKA

Mr A. Schlemmer
FORD WERKE AG
Henry-Ford Strasse 1
D-59735 KÖLN
DEUTSCHLAND

Mr S. Salas
FEDERACIÓN METAL CC. OO
Miembro Comité Empresa General Motors
Fernandez de la Hoz, 12, 2°
E-28010 MADRID
ESPAÑA

Mr P. Schwaiger
REPRESENTATION PERMANENTE DE LA BAVIERE
AUPRES DE L'UNION EUROPEENNE
Counsellor
rue Montoyer 17
B-1040 BRUXELLES
BELGIEN/BELGIQUE/BELGIË

Mr J.E. Sanchez Cuenca
FEDERACIÓN SIDEROMETALURGICA
Secretaria de relaciones internationales
avda. de América 25,5°
E-28008 MADRID
ESPAÑA

Ms K. Schwarzová
METALWORKERSFEDERATION KOVO IN THE SLOVAK
REPUBLIC
International Affairs Department Head
Vajnorska 1
SA-81570 BRATISLAVA
SLOVAK REPUBLIC

Dr R. Soares
PEIRER BARROSO & OLIVEIRA Lda
Director
R. Colegio Sardão, 478
P - 4400 VILA NOVA GAIA
PORTUGAL

Mr S. Sommssich
CELSA S.A.
Executive Vice-President
Ave. Louise, 486
B-1050 BRUXELLES
BELGIEN/BELGIQUE/BELGIË

Mr H. Soboll
DAIMLER-BENZ
Department TEI
TEI
D-70567 MÖHRINGEN (STUTTGART)
DEUTSCHLAND

Mr S.R. Stacey
MALMGREN GOLT KINGSTON & Co
Managing Director
64 Clapham Road
UK-SW9 0JJ LONDON
UNITED KINGDOM

Ms R. Soetaert
EUROPEAN COMMITTEE FOR MOTOR TRADE AND
REPAIRS
General Secretary
Bd de la Woluwe 46 Bte 10
B-1200 BRUSSELS
BELGIEN/BELGIQUE/BELGIË

Ms K. Stauffer
EUROPEAN COMMISSION
Cabinet of Mr Bangemann
Rue de la Loi, 200
B-1049 BRUXELLES
BELGIEN/BELGIQUE/BELGIË

Mr M. Soller
SYNDICAT CGC AUTOMOBILES PEUGEOT SOCHAUX
4, rue Eugène Brunner
F-25600 SOCHAUX CEDEX
FRANCE

Mr F. Stella
EUROPEAN COMMISSION
DG III/E/5
Rue de la Loi, 200
B-1049 BRUSSELS
BELGIEN/BELGIQUE/BELGIË

Ms N. Solyom Demesmay
N. SOLYOM
Consultant in European Public Affairs
24, rue de la Vallée
B-1050 BRUXELLES
BELGIEN/BELGIQUE/BELGIË

Mr Stotko
EUROPEAN AUTOMOTIVE INITIATIVE GROUP
Haager Strasse II
D-84424 ISEN
DEUTSCHLAND

Mr G. Tonini
ITALIAN PERMANENT REPRESENTATION TO THE
EUROPEAN UNION
9, rue du Marteau
B-1040 BRUXELLES
BELGIEN/BELGIQUE/BELGIË

Mr J. Uhlir
ODBOROVY SVAZ KOVO
President
Nam. Churchilla 2
CZ-11359 PRAHA 3
CESKO REPUBLIKA

Dr D. Torchiani
FIAT SpA
rue du Luxembourg 16B
B-1040 BRUXELLES
BELGIEN/BELGIQUE/BELGIË

Mr C. Vallejo
FEDERACIÓN METAL CC. OO
Coordinador Auto F/CC.OO
Fernandez de la Haz, 12, 2°
E-28010 MADRID
ESPAÑA

Mr J. Towers
ROVER GROUP plc
Managing Director
International House
GB-B37 7HQ BIRMINGHAM
UNITED KINGDOM

Mr A. Van Der Haegen
EUROPEAN COMMISSION
Consumer Policy Service
Rue de la Loi, 200
B-1049 BRUXELLES
BELGIEN/BELGIQUE/BELGIË

Dr G. Tripp
BMW AG (PZ)
Director of Central Personnel Department
D - 80788 MÜNCHEN
DEUTSCHLAND

Mr H. Van der Land
INDUSTRIE EN VOEDINGSBOND CNNV
Rietgors 1, Postbus 2080
NL-3430 CK NIEUWEGEIN
NEDERLAND

Mr D. Twynham
GKN AUTOMOTIVE DRIVELINE DIVISION, GKN
AUTOMOTIVR Ltd
Hauptstrasse 150
D-53797 LOHMAR
DEUTSCHLAND

Mr Van Derluis
KUBV
P.O. Box 74800
NL-1070 DM AMSTERDAM
NEDERLAND

Mr L. Vitiello
COMMISSION EUROPEENNE
RP6 - 3/54
Rue de la Loi, 200
B-1049 BRUXELLES
BELGIEN/BELGIQUE/BELGIË

Mr H. Waltersdorfer
BMW AUSTRIA GESELLSCHAFT m.b.H.
General Manager Engine Marketing
Hinterbergerstrasse 2
A-4400 STEYR
ÖSTERREICH

Mr K. Volkert
VOLKSWAGEN AG
D- WOLFSBURG
DEUTSCHLAND

Mr D. Ward
HOUSE OF COMMONS
Policy Adviser to John Smith MP
Westminster
GB-SW1A 8AA LONDON
UNITED KINGDOM

Mr K. Von Holleben
VOLKSWAGEN AG
Haupstabt leiter
Postfach
D-38436 WOLFSBURG
DEUTSCHLAND

Dr D. Waterschoot
CLEPA
Trainee
rue de Stassart 93
B - 1050 BRUXELLES
BELGIEN/BELGIQUE/BELGIË

Mr P. Von Manteuffel
GM EUROPE
Executive Director
Neerveldstraat 107
B-1200 BRUSSEL
BELGIEN/BELGIQUE/BELGIË

Mr D. Watson
TRIPLEX SAFETY GLASS Co Ltd
Sales & Marketing Director
Eckersall Road (Kings Norton)
GB-B38 8SR BIRMINGHAM (WEST MIDLANDS)
UNITED KINGDOM

Mr J.R. Wain
ND MARSTON LTD
Commercial Director
Otley road
GB - BD 17 7 SHIPLEY - WEST YORKSHIRE
UNITED KINGDOM

Mr H. Weirich
VERBAND DER AUTOMOBILINDUSTRIE e.V. (VDA)
Westendastrasse 61
D-60325 FRANKFURT A.M.
DEUTSCHLAND

Mr S. Wright
EUROPEAN INVESTMENT BANK
Senior Economist
100, Bd K. Adenauer
L-2950 LUXEMBOURG
LUXEMBOURG

Mr T. Wynn
EUROPEAN PARLIAMENT
Rue Belliard 97-113
B-1047 BRUXELLES
BELGIEN/BELGIQUE/BELGIË

Mr G. Zohrer
GMBE
Sekretär
Plösselgasse 15
A-1041 WIEN
ÖSTERREICH

SIMULTANEOUS INTERPRETATION WAS PROVIDED BY INTERPRETERS OF THE JOINT
SERVICE INTERPRETATION-CONFERENCES OF THE EUROPEAN COMMISSION

Members of the team

B. BLOCK

M.C. LUX

E. MARZYS

C. MEISSNER

J. OVEJERO

S. ROBERTS

B. SARTA

L. SCHOEBERL

G. TOSITTI

L. VALDIVIA M.

The Automobile Forum was jointly organised by the European Commission and the European Parliament.

EUROPEAN COMMISSION:

Conference Organisation and Techniques Unit of the Joint Services Interpretation-Conferences:

M. Adami
L. Bertrand
B. Delarue
R. Dupont
M. Germano
D. Hespel
D. MacRate
J. Martins
J.P. Scheins
M. Van Asbroek
I. Van Hoorick

Directorate General for Industry

E. Bilson
W. Faber
R. Wright

EUROPEAN PARLIAMENT

C. Tongue, MEP
H. Lewison

European Commission

Forum on the European automobile industry — Written proceedings
Brussels — Palais des Congrès — 1 March 1994

Luxembourg: Office for Official Publications of the European Communities

1994 — VII, 224 pp. — 17.6 x 25.0 cm

ISBN 92-826-8747-3

Price (excluding VAT) in Luxembourg: ECU 8

The European Commission and the European Parliament joined forces to organize a Forum on the European automobile industry, on 1 March 1994 in the Palais des Congrès in Brussels, to provide a platform to discuss key challenges facing the industry. The restructuring process in the industry was examined in detail as well as the responses of the various actors — employers, trade unions and public authorities including the EU — to the transformations underway. The effects of restructuring at regional level and the management of these changes were also discussed. The final workshop, chaired by Ms C. Tongue, MEP, examined ways to enhance partnership and cooperation in the industry and among the social partners concerned. In addition, there was an opening address given by Mr M. Bangemann, a Member of the European Commission, and Professor R. Blanpain gave an independent summary speech to close the Forum. This publication is a transcript of the whole Forum, and also includes the workshop summaries and reports.